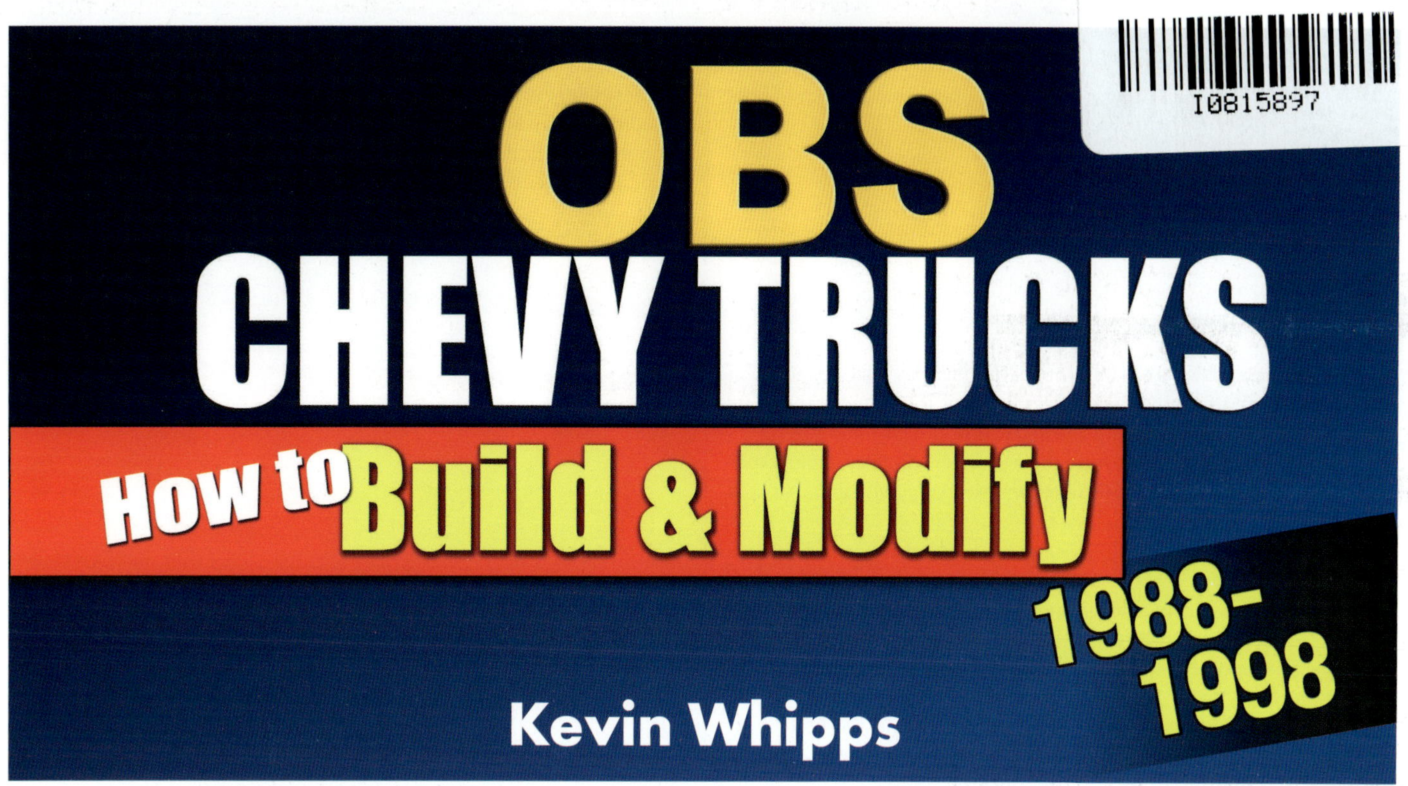

OBS
CHEVY TRUCKS
How to Build & Modify
1988-1998
Kevin Whipps
I0815897

SA
S-A DESIGN

OFFICIAL TRUCK

CarTech®

CarTech®

CarTech®, Inc.
6118 Main Street
North Branch, MN 55056
Phone: 651-277-1200 or 800-551-4754
Fax: 651-277-1203
www.cartechbooks.com

Edit by Bob Wilson
Layout by Ella Nordrum

ISBN 978-1-61325-767-8
Item No. SA536

Library of Congress Cataloging-in-Publication Data Available

Written, edited, and designed in the U.S.A.
Printed in China
10 9 8 7 6 5 4 3 2 1

DISTRIBUTION BY:

Europe
PGUK
63 Hatton Garden
London EC1N 8LE, England
Phone: 020 7061 1980 • Fax: 020 7242 3725
www.pguk.co.uk

Australia
Renniks Publications Ltd.
3/37-39 Green Street
Banksmeadow, NSW 2109, Australia
Phone: 2 9695 7055 • Fax: 2 9695 7355
www.renniks.com

Canada
Login Canada
300 Saulteaux Crescent
Winnipeg, MB, R3J 3T2 Canada
Phone: 800 665 1148 • Fax: 800 665 0103
www.lb.ca

CONTENTS

DEDICATION

For Murray.

ACKNOWLEDGMENTS

Books such as this one aren't easy to write. You need to talk to what seems like a million different people, coordinate your schedule with theirs, and find a way to get something done together. Sometimes things work out and sometimes they do not. Fortunately, I've met a lot of cool people while doing these books, and I know who to turn to when I need help. To everyone who helped me with this project, whether you're mentioned on these pages or not, thank you. You're all appreciated.

Seth at Switch Suspension is one of those guys. I've known him for what seems like forever. We've tag-teamed articles for magazines and previous projects, and he came through again for this book. Since part of it was written during the COVID-19 pandemic, I couldn't go to his shop any time that I wanted. Instead, he took his own pictures and sent them to me. He's a very generous man, and I'm always grateful for his help.

In one sense, this book wouldn't be possible without people like Jose "Cougar" Velasco. He runs @C10Sales on Instagram, and not only is he the reason that I constantly find new projects but he's also the person who sold me the one that's referenced in this book: my 1997 Chevrolet Centurion. In addition, if I needed a part, I just had to ask him to keep his feelers out, and he'd come through. He's a good man to know and a great person to follow on Instagram.

I met Lonnie Thompson from Carolina Kustoms in Portland, Oregon, when I went there to get photos for my first book, *How to Restore Your Chevy Truck: 1973–1987*. Since then, if I've ever needed anything, he's sent me a download link, and we've been good to go. When I just mentioned this book to him, he sent me a whole ton of shots. He's clutch, and I appreciate that.

Ronnie Wetch, from the C10 Talk podcast, is the person who I call when I need the answer to an obscure question. I can ask, "Hey Ronnie, what year did they put those mirrors in that weird place?" He'll have the answer. In addition, he's a friend. If I need a hand wrenching in the garage or just someone to lend an ear, he's there. Check out his other podcast, OBS Talk, to catch up on all things 1988–1998.

I met Jim Pickering in person at the Specialty Equipment Marketing Association (SEMA) Show, but before that, he reached out to me via my website to get some support for his first book, *Chevy/GMC Trucks 1973–1987: How to Build & Modify*. I had just finished my first book and was working on my second, and we were able to help each other. Soon, we became buddies. Now, he's the person who I call if I need help with something technical or if I just want to talk. After all, us writers who work on car books are not very common. Someday, I hope to move to the Portland, Oregon, area where he lives. Then, I'll really annoy him.

Let's talk about my buddy, Ruben Castañon, who is also known as @wheel_snob on Instagram. I met him when I lived in Tucson, Arizona, and I was selling a set of seats from my Centurion. We've become friends since that time, and many of the photos in the paint chapter came from his camera. He has a killer crew-cab, short-bed dually, and if you need some old-school billet wheels, he's your guy. He's also a great person to follow on Instagram, so give him a shout.

ABOUT THE AUTHOR

In 1999, Kevin Whipps began writing feature articles for national automotive magazines. He then transitioned to roles as a copy editor, editor, executive editor, and editor in chief. He is the author of the following books: *How to Restore Your Chevy Truck: 1973–1987*, *How to Restore Your Chevy Truck: 1967–1972*, and *How to Install Air Ride Suspension*. In addition, he does marketing and ghostwriting work for various clients.

When he's not working, Whipps spends time with his children, KJ and Kaylee. If he's not doing that, he's reading comic books or wrenching on projects in his garage. He lives in the Phoenix, Arizona, area.

INTRODUCTION

The year 2008 wasn't a great time for someone to start a new job. Yet, there I was, just a month after my wedding, beginning a new gig as a copy editor for a local fashion magazine. My wife had been laid off from her job the previous week, and my new job came with a slight pay cut. However, it was something that was at least adjacent to writing, so she encouraged me to take the position.

At the time, I had four project vehicles—well, five, technically. So, I started selling them. I sold my 2001 GMC that was channeled with suicide doors and a four-pump hydraulic setup to my friend, Aaron Garcia. His son, Tyler, finished the truck, and now I see shots of it on Instagram.

My 2004 Silverado was also channeled, but this one had been completed. It made two appearances at SEMA and featured 22-inch Bonspeed wheels, a suede interior, and a Porsche blue paint job. It was a show truck that I often drove while I ran errands. I loved that vehicle, but when someone handed me a bunch of cash, I took it.

I had two Squarebody trucks at the time: a 1984 truck named *Steve II* (the original *Steve* was sold years before) and a crew-cab dually. Both of them were sold to my friends for inexpensive prices. Also during this time frame, I sold a 1952 Chevy truck, which until that point was the only vehicle that I ever sold for a profit.

I sold the trucks because I needed money, and this was a quick way to get some. However, I still needed a way to get to work, particularly while my wife used our other car to find a job. I called my buddy Scott Renner and offered to buy his dad's 1995 Chevrolet Silverado. It was white, lowered slightly, and had the 5.7L engine. It was perfect.

Nostalgia is a powerful thing.

I began high school in 1990. Although I lived in a middle-class neighborhood, my classmates came from all over the city—often from wealthy parts of town. So, when I turned 16 years old in 1992, I took possession of a 1988 Daihatsu Charade, while my friends received new trucks. For them, that was often a 1992 (or 1993) Chevrolet Silverado, and it was probably customized too.

There was one kid who was maybe 5-foot, 3-inches tall that pulled up one day in a truck that his folks had purchased for him. It was a black full-size, extra-cab Chevy that was painted with white ovals up front (just like a killer whale), and it had two purple streaks between the white and the black. It was lowered on 15- or 16-inch wheels, and I was pretty sure that I had seen it a few months back in an issue of *Sport Truck* magazine. It was beautiful—so much more than my 3-cylinder car. I wanted one so bad.

That kid and his truck stuck with me for a long time.

In 2009, my buddy Todd from Lowboy Motorsports and I (mostly Todd) bagged and body dropped my new-to-me 1995 truck. I drove it to work every day while working at the fashion magazine.

Later in 2009, I began freelancing full time. Two years later, my wife had gone through another two jobs, and I had to sell the 1995 truck. People here in Arizona were hit pretty hard by the Great Recession, and my truck was the only big item that we had left to sell. It had to go, so it did. A guy who I knew paid way too little for it, with the promise that he'd finish the truck. He didn't. Instead, he flipped it for some quick cash, and last I heard, someone in Colorado owned it.

Now, I've built many cars and trucks in my day. My rides have graced a few covers, and without them, I wouldn't be writing this book today. However, that 1995 Chevy was something special, and it changed me a lot.

It was the last custom vehicle that I'd build.

I profoundly miss that truck. You'd think that I'd miss the car that got me my first writing gig, the one that was shot for the cover of a magazine with a model, or my 2004, which was the truck that I drove home from SEMA to attend my sister's funeral. However, it's that white 1995 truck that I think about almost daily. The interior had a blue dash and tan seats. The GMC grille looked good, but the bumper was trash. In addition, it needed a paint job. Despite this, it was so much fun to drive, and I never worried about it. Even looking at photos of it as I write this book, I think about how great it would be to have one again.

Essentially, that 1995 Chevy was my white whale—until recently.

Before I signed the contract to write this book, I had been scheming of a way to get a ride like my 1995 truck. Previous editors told me to never buy a project just for a book because it always takes too long to build. However, I wanted my 1995 truck again. Book or no book, I wanted a project in my garage, and it was going to happen. I sold the 1981 Silverado that I bought to finish my first book, *How to Restore Your Chevy Truck: 1973–1987*, and looked on Craigslist, OfferUp, Facebook Marketplace, and Instagram to find something, anything, that would solve my problem. Then, I found it.

There's a guy named Jose in the Long Beach, California, area who everyone calls "Cougar." He runs @C10Sales on Instagram, and we've chatted over the years. I once entered a raffle that he was having for a Squarebody dually, and even though I lost, I won a consolation prize: a cordless 3/8-inch Snap-on impact wrench. So, when he posted one of his personal vehicles, I looked. It was out of my price range, but after talking to him about it, we worked out a deal. So, in the middle of a pandemic, I hopped on a plane to Long Beach and drove my prize home.

The truck is a 1997 Chevrolet Silverado. Although that seems pretty standard, this one is definitely not. It's a Centurion, which is a crew-cab, short-bed, 1/2-ton Silverado. Centurion (the now-defunct company) built these things using General Motors parts in the late 1990s, and they're super rare. Mine has a ton of miles on it and a few problems, but it made the 9-hour drive home.

The truck was still new to me at this point, so my plans weren't cemented quite yet. I knew that I wanted to lower it farther and throw 22-inch wheels on it for a little while, and the plan eventually involved airbags and a body drop. However, for the immediate moment, I just wanted a clean and relatively pretty cruiser. I wouldn't touch the chipped paint and wouldn't go too nuts on the outside, but I cleaned up everything that I could. Of course, I documented it all for this book. That was part of the reason for buying the truck, after all.

When I hit the halfway point of writing this book, things changed again. I owned a 2019 Chevrolet Silverado at the time, and the dealership offerred to buy it back for about $1,000 less than the price that I bought it for new. So, I sold it. With the change left over after paying it off, I bought another one of my dream trucks: a 1998 two-door, two-wheel-drive Chevrolet Tahoe. It has a tick over 118,000 miles on the odometer, and it's in pretty good shape.

Neither the crew cab nor the Tahoe are my 1995 truck, and they never will be. Back then, I didn't have kids, so there was no reason to have a back seat. Today, with the Centurion and the Tahoe, I have room for both of my children, a few subwoofers, and two more if I want to cram them inside.

These trucks are the right ones for me at this point in my life. I suppose that's what I'm getting at here in this long-winded introduction. The right truck for you is out there somewhere. It could be an extra-cab long-bed that you want to use to haul parts around and make you look cool or a full-blown SEMA Show feature vehicle that garners a ton of attention.

My goal with this book is to help you determine what kind of build you want to do and then execute that vision. Since there's such a wide spectrum of projects out there, this isn't a simple challenge. However, I'm hopeful that the results will be worth it.

I want to see your projects too. Feel free to tag me on Instagram (@kevinwhipps) to show me your cool trucks. I can't wait to see what you build.

CHAPTER 1

The History of 1988–1998 Chevy Trucks

In 1988, Chevrolet introduced its latest truck model: a C/K 1500. The "C" referred to the two-wheel-drive models, and the "K" stood for the four-wheel-drive models. Internally, this was the GMT400 platform. At the same time, Chevrolet was still producing the Suburban, Blazer, 3/4-ton truck, and 1-ton truck from the previous generation. This meant that the Squarebody trucks (the nickname given to 1973–1987 Chevy and GMC full-size pickups) were on the sales floor along with the new models. It was weird, but it must've worked because General Motors did the same thing in 1999.

The new C/K was a pretty truck. Previous generations weren't as focused on leg room, and the stretched cab certainly helped with that. There was also the introduction of an extended-cab option, which was the first of its kind for Chevrolet and its full-size pickups. Although, it was only available on the fleetside models at first. The viewing area was improved, as there was a lot more glass.

Those are the basic details. Let's go into the year-by-year specific details.

1988

The C/K model was introduced in 1988. There are fleetsides, stepsides (sometimes called sportsides), extended cabs, standard cabs, and three Chevy trim levels: Cheyenne (base), Scottsdale, and Silverado. Meanwhile, GMC had the base, SLX, and SLE. The higher trim levels (Scottsdale, Silverado, SLX, and SLE) typically came with four individual headlights, while the lower models came with a single, sealed-beam lens. Three engine options were available: the 4.3L V-6, 5.0L V-8 (305 ci), and 5.7L V-8 (350 ci). Other engines were options for the more heavy-duty trucks, but only those three were available for the 1/2-ton.

1989

A sport appearance package was introduced in 1989 for Chevrolet and GMC trucks. With the Chevys, it was available only on the fleetside model, and it had a body-colored grille, sport graphics (it literally had a "SPORT" decal on the back of the bed), body-colored bumpers, chrome wheels, and fog lights. The Sierra had the same basic features but was called the Sierra GT.

This 1990 Chevrolet Sport is a clean example of the trucks of the 1988–1998 era. (Photo Courtesy Switch Suspension)

1990

The 1990 model year featured the introduction of the 454 SS, which was painted Onyx Black and had the same options and trim as the Silverado. The 454 motor made 230 hp and a whopping 385 ft-lbs of torque. Chevrolet also introduced the W/T model, which was a regular-cab, long-bed truck that was stripped of most options. It was basically a Cheyenne with a different grille and headlights, plus black bumpers. The Scottsdale, Silverado, SLX, and SLE models now received composite headlights that were the same basic shape as the four individual models but in one housing.

1991

Although there wasn't much to announce in 1991 regarding light-duty trucks, this was the year that General Motors released its 1-ton dually and an updated 454 engine. In addition, the 4L80E automatic transmission was introduced, but you could only find it on heavy-duty models. Options for a tachometer, bedliner, and reclining bucket seats were now available as well.

1992

In 1992, you could order a stepside pickup with an extended cab, which was a first for General Motors. The automaker also added red and white as color options for the 454 SS. This is also when General Motors updated the Suburbans and 3/4- and 1-ton trucks (in crew cabs) to the current platform.

1993

A Sport edition for stepsides was introduced in 1993. It had the same basic options, except it had cast-aluminum wheels instead of chrome. General Motors updated the 4.3L V-6 and ditched the Scottsdale trim level. This was the last year that the 454 SS was offered.

1994

In 1994, General Motors worked on the big changes that would be implemented in 1995. The grilles on the Chevy and the GMC models shifted to the appearance that lasted until the end of the bodystyle. The GMCs also added an SLT trim level as a top-of-the-line version, and the base was renamed the SL.

1995

It was a big year for General Motors in 1995. The interior of the truck was changed from the previous boxy version to be more comfortable and ergonomic. A driver-side airbag and four-wheel antilock braking system (ABS) were added. This is what most people consider to be the dividing year in the bodystyle, meaning the point in which everything was mildly redesigned.

1996

The Vortec line of engines was introduced in 1996. Every gas engine (the 4.3L V-6, 5.0L V-8, and 5.7L V-8) gained central sequential fuel injection. The Vortec system was all about new heads that provided a higher

The grille and the dash indicate that this stepside/sportside truck is a pre-1994 model.

This is the 5.7L Vortec V-8 engine that was used in General Motors trucks and SUVs of the era. (Photo Courtesy Switch Suspension)

compression ratio, more horsepower, more torque, and better airflow. It also came with OBD-II, a system that lets consumers and mechanics plug into a diagnostic port under the driver-side knee panel on the dash. In addition, daytime running lights became standard, and if you had an extended cab, you could get an optional third door.

1997

In 1997, the 1/2-ton truck received a passenger-side airbag. The power-steering system was upgraded to an electronic speed-sensitive setup, and the transmissions (4L60E and 4L80E) were adjusted for improved efficiency and better shifting.

1998

The last year for the 1/2-tons was in 1998, so the only changes were the additions of OnStar as an option and a Passlock theft-deterrent system.

Differences: 1988–1994 versus 1995–1998

These trucks can be separated into two basic groups: 1988–1994 and 1995–1998. With both of them, there are two changes to note.

The minor changes happened to the exterior. Not much changed overall from a sheet-metal perspective. A 1998 Silverado has the same hood as a 1988 model, and the basic appearance of the trucks is the same. Most of the changes were regarding the paint colors and the front end, specifically the grille.

Chevy and GMC featured grille updates for the 1994 model. The GMC version had the biggest change, as the marker lights were pushed up higher into the facia. The Chevys had a bit more of a rounded look. It's definitely subtle. The only other major exterior change was the addition of a third door for extended-cab models in 1996.

The major change came first in the form of the interior. This was a huge difference between the two trucks. While the 1988–1994 models had a squared-off dashboard and interior, the new look from 1995 onward was rounded and relatively sleek. There were very few hard corners or edges integrated into the design, and it was even easier to install a stereo without all sorts of leftover components stuck in the dash.

The second major change dealt with the engine. General Motors moved into the Vortec era, going away from the throttle-body fuel injection (TBI) of previous years. There are plenty of debates about whether or not Vortec was an improvement, but it was a huge change in the way that these trucks performed, even if it didn't seem that way on the surface.

What does of this all mean for you and your truck purchase?

Think about the aspects of the truck that are important to you. For example, begin with the cab: do you want a standard cab or an extended cab? For the sake of argument, say that you want an extended cab. Now, select the

Forums and the Rise of the "OBS"

While researching the 1988–1998 Chevy and GMC trucks, you'll often come across the acronym "OBS." However, what it means may not make sense unless you were on the truck forum websites in the early 2000s.

At that time, several web forums catered to the General Motors truck market. One of the staples for older truck builders is 67-72chevytrucks.com, which has expanded well past its domain name's years. There was also GMFullsize.com and FullsizeChevy.com, both of which shared members and were dedicated to trucks (mostly newer models).

This is where the problem began. At the time, the 1999 Silverado was relatively new. Usually, people group a model of truck by the years: 1967–1972, 1973–1987, etc. However, there was no end date at the time for the 1999-and-newer trucks, so forum contributors needed a term to designate the bodystyle. What they came up with was "New Body Style" (NBS). The name stuck, and from that point forward, the General Motors bodystyle of trucks that began in 1999 was known as the NBS trucks.

By that logic, anything prior to 1999 would be an old body style. Since the 1988–1998 trucks were the previous generation, they became known as Old Body Style (OBS) trucks. The name stuck, and today there's everything from magazines to podcasts with the OBS moniker.

However, there was another interesting twist. When Chevy released the 2007–2014 models, it didn't extend things forward with NBS becoming OBS and so on. People who owned the 1999–2007 classic models didn't want to give up their nickname. Instead, they called those trucks the "New New Body Style" (NNBS). Although, it didn't take hold like OBS or NBS. ■

bed: do you want a stepside/sportside or a fleetside? Okay, stepside it is. Pick between the two major changes in the truck with 1988–1994 and 1995–1998. If you want the older model, technically you need to get a 1992–1994 truck because General Motors didn't offer an extended-cab stepside model until 1992. However, if you go with a newer model, you're good.

That, in essence, is the process. Except for things such as special models and the like, narrow down what kind of truck you want as a base and fine-tune your results based on what you can find, afford, and buy.

Options

When selecting a truck, there are anywhere from two to three different trim levels from which to choose. Cheyenne, Scottsdale, and Silverado are the Chevrolet trim levels. GMC has the base, SLX, and SLE. Any project will be cheaper with one of the lower trim levels. If the goal is to swap out the engine, it may be a better choice. However, higher-end models come with options such as power windows, and those can make a big difference in the convenience and drivability of the truck.

Models

The Chevrolet and GMC truck models are below.

W/T

The Work Truck (W/T) model, means that it's as stripped down as possible. This trim levels was introduced in 1990, and if you find one, it will be pretty simple. The W/T had vinyl floors, window cranks, and an AM/FM stereo (assuming that it has not been modified). They had the single headlamps up front and usually a plastic grille that's black in color.

Cheyenne

The Cheyenne was the base-model truck that's just above the W/T. It was the most visually different from the rest. The front end was the obvious part, as it had two single sealed-beam headlamps instead of the four lamps that were found in earlier models.

Scottsdale

Scottsdale model trucks were made only from 1988 to 1991, so there's a smaller selection from which to choose. There's a reason for that. The differences between the Silverado and Scottsdale were minimal, and, eventually, the Silverado won out. Basic features included the "Scottsdale" nameplate on the B-pillar and black plastic bodyside moldings. The interior was a bit nicer than the Cheyenne, though, with a standard cloth bench and similar options.

Silverado

This was *the* truck. It was the one with all power options available—from power steering to a tilt column and everything in between. Most came with a 350 V-8, and some even had two-tone paint jobs. This was the one with all of the bells and whistles, and it was usually the option that most people wanted.

GMCs

As a general rule of thumb, GMC models tend to have more options at lower levels, even though sometimes it just comes down to paint or upholstery. Regardless, they had a few different options as well.

SL

GMC never had the W/T model, as that name was only used by Chevy. Instead, the SL was GMC's take on the Cheyenne. That meant that it was the base-model truck, and it had options such as manual windows and the like.

SLX

The SLX was GMC's equivalent to Chevrolet's Scottsdale, and it was discontinued after the 1991 model year.

SLE

While Chevy had the Silverado, GMC had the SLE. It had the four sealed-beam headlights and the like, plus all of the power options. However, with the 1994 refresh, the GMC grille improved substantially, and it is now considered a more desirable option for some Chevy truck owners.

1988–1994 versus 1995–1998

As with most of today's vehicles, there was a refresh of the bodystyle midway through the OBS's production run. There are a few various items to note here, and this is where things get really interesting. Some years have very specific features, while others are the same all the way around.

The big change in 1994 was made to the front end, and that was the only difference between these trucks and the previous models. The grille is the most noticeable shift, which on the GMCs involved raising the parking lamps and insetting the center grille slightly. Chevy trucks had a more rounded front grille, which was also a cleaner look. So, if you want a truck with the older dash but the newer front end, a 1994 model fulfills both requirements.

Many big changes came with the 1995 model year. The mirrors were adapted from the Suburbans to become universal across all sport utility vehicles (SUVs) and trucks. The

This 1993 model has the older, more square dashboard. (Photo Courtesy Jeff Volker)

This dashboard is in a 1997 Silverado, and it has the passenger-side airbag.

interior changed dramatically, with a new rounded dashboard (that is prone to cracking) and door panels. In addition, it featured a new center console and seats. Even older truck owners search for these newer parts to install them into their trucks.

Unique to 1995 and 1996 was the dashboard. In 1997, passenger-side airbags became standard, and the dash changed as a result. While the 1995 and 1996 models had shallow cupholders that do very little to actually hold a drink in place, it overall looks a bit cleaner and is easier to upholster. Meanwhile, the 1997 dashboard had a dip and a new hump on the side to accommodate the airbag, which is a design that not everyone loves.

The 1996 model introduced a third door for the extended-cab trucks, which was a huge deal at the time. This gave the truck a crew cab–like appeal but without the extra length. In addition, it was possible to get a 60/40 bench in the Silverado, where a center armrest and console pivoted down from the middle area. Today, these consoles are a bit finicky and can break, keeping them stuck in either the up or the down positions.

The 1997 model included the aforementioned passenger-side airbag—but only on the 1500- and 2500-series trucks. The 3500-series trucks (the duallies) typically had the newer dashboard, but instead of the airbag, they had a pocket. Some customizers prefer the pocket to the airbag, and they install a screen of some sort in there too.

Interior Options

The interior of these trucks changed dramatically in 1995. Previously, it had been fairly boxy. It could be compared to the previous generation of Chevy trucks (1973–1987) with straight door panels and power window switches that were less than ergonomic. Everything was very angular for the 1988–1994 models. While there was a period of time when it didn't look great, it has aged well.

The 1995 model year has a very rounded look to the inside. The dash had a 1.5-DIN stereo cutout, which car stereo manufacturers of the era used as an excuse to build 1.5-DIN decks. (The acronym DIN stands for Deutsches Institut für Normung, which is the German organization for standardization.) The 1995 and 1996 models had a driver-side airbag, and the passenger's side received one as well in 1997.

Although the 1995–1998 dashboards look great, they have a big problem: they crack (as do 1989–1994s, but it's typically worse with the newer models). It's difficult to find a dashboard of that era in decent shape. Some are even shattered behind the stereo. Cracks can often be found around the dash bezel or near the vents. Hairline cracks may take some time to locate, but they will show up eventually.

What's the solution? Well, there isn't much of one. It is possible to try to fuse the panels together with epoxy or a plastic repair product. However, the most difficult task is matching the texture on the top. It can be painted to match the truck (smoothing it out so that it doesn't need texture); replaced with something custom; or wrapped in fabric.

The dashboard in this 1998 model has the passenger-side airbag. In addition, it has no cracks, which is rare.

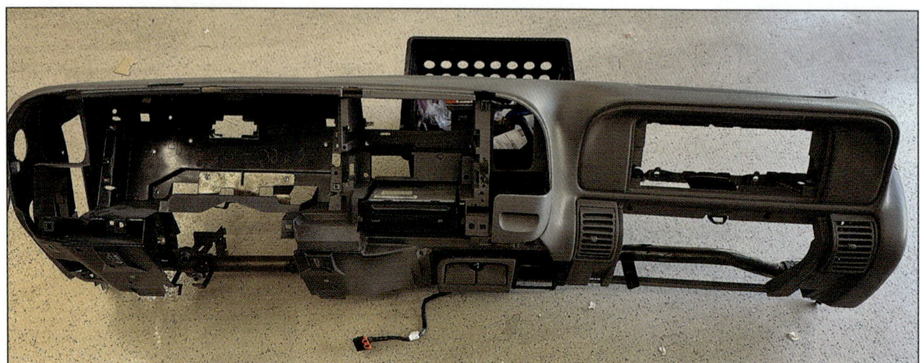

If you find a spare dashboard, buy it. Even if yours isn't cracked now, it may crack in the future, and the $300 investment isn't bad.

Some aftermarket manufacturers provide options for the earlier models, but the jury is still out regarding the quality.

Truck Design

While the 1988–1998 Chevy and GMC trucks are called OBSs today, General Motors calls them the GMT400 platform. Alternatively, they are known as C/K pickups from Chevy (the K version is for four-wheel-drive models) and Sierra pickups from GMC.

When compared to the 1973–1987 trucks, which have been nicknamed "squarebodies" by their fans, OBS trucks are practically aerodynamic wonders with curved body panels and a more rounded overall appearance. They have flush window glass, no more vent windows, and many other aspects that set them apart from their predecessors.

The big item that must be covered is the extended cab. This was a first for GM trucks. While the competition had offered an extended cab for about 15 years by 1988, when it finally came to Chevrolet and GMC, consumers were ecstatic. It was a welcome addition to a popular line of trucks. The addition of the third door was icing on the cake.

The *Sport Truck* Era

In 1988, General Motors introduced its new line of pickups. At the same time, something new appeared on newsstands: *Sport Truck* magazine. It was all about the performance and show arenas for trucks, and it was extremely popular.

Around this same time, people (such as Boyd Coddington) were getting their hands on these pickups and turning them into something cool.

This is Sport Truck magazine right before it was shuttered in 2009. The publication operated for more than 20 years, and it made a profound impact on the truck scene.

The Centurion

Crew-cab pickups are common today, and they were common in 1988 as well. However, they were only available on 3/4-ton and 1-ton models (not on the 1/2 ton). So, to carry four people comfortably in the truck, the only option was to buy something heavy duty. This meant that you'd probably have to get a long bed, which made for a very large vehicle.

This 1997 Centurion is a Chevy, but it has a GMC front grille. It is a true 1/2-ton short-bed truck, and production numbers were low.

In 1996, that changed. Centurion Vehicles, Inc., a company that was purchased by Southern Comfort in 2006, built a limited run of short-bed, crew-cab trucks in two- and four-wheel-drive, 1/2-, 3/4-, and 1-ton models. However, it didn't produce many of them. Information is difficult to find, but it's likely that no more than 40 were made each of those years, and fewer than 150 were built overall. So, if you can find one, you've found a unicorn with hen's teeth.

Conversion companies can have a bad reputation, but in this case, the trucks were built with all parts from General Motors. As the stories go, they used a standard-cab truck as a base, swapped the cab with a General Motors crew cab, and filled it up with all General Motors parts. (Some say that Centurion stretched the cab by cutting and splicing in a crew-cab aft section, but a physical examination indicates that was not the case.) The frame was lengthened 37 inches and cut in a distinctive diagonal pattern, which, although it's not the strongest way to make that kind of joint, seems to have worked out for some of the people who still own them. Basically, it looks just like the truck that General Motors would build years later but with 1996–1998 styling.

The frame looks stock, but there is an angled cut in the middle to stretch out what was a standard cab. In addition, the mount is not stock. It's from a Centurion.

Today, some people attempt to recreate the Centurion, and they go about it in various ways. Some buy a 3/4- or 1-ton truck, cut down the frame to accept a short bed, and modify the suspension to suit their needs. Others go a similar route that Centurion did by purchasing a good crew-cab body and then stretching their existing standard- or extra-cab truck. Either way, the process requires a substantial amount of work, but the results can be great.

If you find a Centurion for sale, scoop it up. Even if you don't want to build it, the truck may be worth a significant amount of money in the future. ■

This Centurion dually is owned by Ruben Castañon of Casa Grande, Arizona. Today, it's bagged and on those same wheels. (Photo Courtesy Ruben Castañon)

Whether they chopped the top or just installed billet wheels, it was a modification, and people were eating it up. *Sport Truck* sold well every month because it always had a cool contemporary truck on the cover that was usually lowered on BellTech products and featured paint by artists such as Mike Learn. It was an amazing time.

This led to an explosion in aftermarket parts for these trucks. Shops such as Empire Motorsports and Traders sprung up to fill the demand, and it seemed like there was a new vendor opening every other week that pumped out billet parts. In Arizona, Truck Creations by Verdone was a huge contributor to the scene, landing quite a few *Sport Truck* covers in the process.

There's a lot to unpack about the

1993 Indianapolis 500 Pace Truck Edition

Many special-edition Chevy and GMC trucks exist, but one that gets a lot of attention is the 1993 Chevrolet Silverado Indianapolis 500 Pace Truck edition.

Only 1,235 of these trucks were built, and it was for a relatively obscure anniversary: 77 years of the Indianapolis 500. However, it's pretty, so it's a good truck to buy.

It has the custom graphics down the sides and official badging. The front bumper has large vents that were previously only available on the diesel models and make quite the visual statement. There's also a color-matched grille and front clip—plus, it has fog lights. It comes standard with a 350 V-8.

Customizing one of these trucks may seem like blasphemy, but that's also what makes it so cool—it's the forbidden fruit. In fact, there's a build of one in this very book. The owner wanted a set of coilovers, new wheels, and bigger brakes, and the shop delivered. ■

This 1993 Indy truck is owned by Jeff Volker. It was built on a Roadster Shop Low-Pro chassis and has all of the goodies. (Photo Courtesy Jeff Volker)

This truck lays out flat without needing to cut the bed floor and still has all of the creature comforts. (Photo Courtesy Jeff Volker)

The level of detail on this truck is amazing. Look closely at those air tanks. They have the same Indy graphics as the rest of the truck. (Photo Courtesy Jeff Volker)

The 454 SS

Of all 1988–1998 Chevy and GMC trucks, the 1990–1993 454 SS has been called the Holy Grail, and it's not difficult to understand why.

If it's not obvious from the name, the truck came with a 454-ci big-block V-8. That engine was shoved into a relatively lightweight standard-cab truck chassis, so the gobs of available torque could put down some mean rubber on the track or the street. In 1990, this truck had 383 ft-lbs of torque but only 230 hp. That combination of torque and weight gave it a 7.7-second 0-to-60 time. That, and they were a lot of fun to do burnouts in.

The 1991 model year brought a 25-hp upgrade to the 454, increasing it to 255 hp. In addition, the transmission was upgraded, switching from a Turbo Hydra-matic to a 4L80E. These upgrades shaved off a half second from the 0-to-60 time, which was now 7.2 seconds. Later models usually ran the quarter mile in about 15.7 seconds.

Only 16,953 454 SS trucks were built. Most of them were built for the 1990 model year (13,748 produced), and in 1990 and 1991, the only color option was Onyx Black with a Garnet Red interior. In 1992 and 1993, Summit White or Victory Red were available for the exterior colors in addition to Onyx Black. Since General Motors only made 3,205 of these trucks in 1991, 1992, and 1993, it's pretty difficult to find a red or white one in decent shape. In addition, no matter what you find, these trucks are usually not cheap.

While the Centurion is rarer, it's not very well known. The Indy Pace Truck is out there, but aside from the graphics, it's not particularly special. However, the 454 SS was part of a series of muscle trucks that was released in the early 1990s and spurned the sport truck market's growth. It's an icon, and people expect to sell them for a pretty penny. Bring your pocketbook if you want one.

Although they are difficult to find for a decent price and may be a tick overrated, they get a lot of attention at a show. If you're the lucky owner of one, these trucks have a lot of potential value. ■

The Two-Door Tahoe

From 1969 to 1990, General Motors built the Blazer, a truck that was (and is) extremely popular with the four-wheel-drive crowd. They're regularly lifted with big wheels and tires and taken out to the desert, looking killer as they do so. Even their two-wheel-drive brethren gets a lot of attention because they look good when they're dropped. So, when Chevy refreshed the lineup with the OBS trucks, a Blazer was in the cards.

Although the 1991–1995 Blazers and Yukons are cool, there wasn't a two-door, two-wheel-drive version. Sales of the four-door models dominated the two-doors, particularly for families. That made the whole line a little bit less cool too.

So, in 1996, General Motors introduced the Chevrolet Tahoe with a two-door, two-wheel-drive model. It was only made until 2000, but it made an impact in those five model years.

These trucks look amazing when they're laid out. They're similar to standard-cab trucks, but they are shorter and have a tighter turning radius. They were available in two styles: with barn doors in the back or with a hatch and tailgate.

There's a lot to talk about with these trucks, which is one of the reasons why they're in this book. Although

Castañon's Tahoe sits in front of a pair of palm trees. (Photo Courtesy Ruben Castañon)

The Two-Door Tahoe *continued*

The two-door Tahoe looks great on 22-inch wheels, including these US Mags, which look similar to the stock 454 wheels. (Photo Courtesy Switch Suspension)

they're popular, they're also rare enough that they don't warrant a book of their own. However, since they have so much in common with the regular trucks, and they're so popular with this crowd, it makes sense to cover them here.

These trucks are all on the same platform, and the methods applied to one apply to the others too. The only exceptions are when it comes to things like gas tank placement, certain rear suspension swaps, and everything in the interior behind the front seats. Otherwise everything is the same including the basic techniques. ■

The roll pan on the back of this Tahoe looks good. (Photo Courtesy Ruben Castañon)

Sport Truck era, and it could all be done in its own book. Here's what you, the consumer, need to know.

First, because these trucks were so huge in the sport truck scene, they're really popular, particularly with folks born in the 1970s who may have owned one as their first truck or just lusted after them in the magazines. Those people are older now, which means that they likely have enough money to purchase one on their own, which also means that these trucks will not decrease in price any time soon.

Second, there is a huge opportunity with this build that can't be found with other trucks: building something that is period correct.

Before the *Sport Truck* era, magazines such as *Truckin'* and others existed. However, in the 1970s and 1980s, a lot of the popular stuff included lifted trucks and, believe it or not, vans. It's difficult to go back into one of those books and find enough data to see what was cool or not in a particular year. In the 1990s, among *Sport Truck*, *Truckin'*, and, later in the decade, *Street Trucks*, thousands of pages of data are waiting. *Truckin'* alone used to be close to 300 pages every month.

So, if you want to build something that looks like it came right off the line in 1994 and was driven to a Trader's store to get parts, you have a lot of research to do. However, it is all possible, which makes this avenue a pretty popular one to take. There have been quite a few appearances of old *Sport Truck* cover trucks at recent shows, and you could make your own facsimile if you wanted to.

CHAPTER 2

Finding the Right Truck

What kind of 1988–1998 Chevy or GMC truck do you want to build? This seems like a simple question, but it's not. Is it okay to get a work truck? Should you buy a vehicle that's in great shape or one that needs some extra love?

Builds can range from a mild custom with only bolt-on parts to a show winner that can be taken to a major event, or be on the cover of a national magazine. There is a wide range of options from which to choose, and it directly affects the type of truck that you should buy.

For example, let's say that you have a connection with a painter or maybe you plan to paint the truck yourself. You could buy a truck with rust, body damage, and maybe some other issues and be fine. As long as it runs, you're set. If you want to install a 6.0L LS engine under the hood, buying a Cheyenne with a 4.3L V-6 is just fine because you plan to swap the motor anyway.

So, before making a purchase, determine what you want the end result to be. Let's begin by broadly defining the options.

Bolt-On Custom

A bolt-on custom is exactly what it sounds like: a truck that is built using primarily bolt-on parts. There are no body modifications that involve paint or bodywork. They can all be accomplished by turning a wrench.

Would a vinyl wrap count? Sure. Is an engine swap in this category? Technically, yes. Basically, a bolt-on custom is a vehicle where welding isn't involved and the barrier to entry low.

Mild Custom

Truck shows regularly classify trucks based on the number of body modifications that have been performed. A mild custom has one-to-five body modifications. That usually includes shaving the tailgate, adding a roll pan, etc. It's a custom truck, but it's not a full-blown custom truck.

This truck can be classified between a bolt-on custom and a mild custom. It has custom paint—but only in that the top was sprayed black over the factory white. Otherwise, there are no other major modifications. (Photo Courtesy Switch Suspension)

Full Custom

A full custom is a truck that has many body modifications, a full paint job, and maybe even some graphics. It's a custom truck, and you can still drive it—or you could if you wanted to. This isn't a trailer-queen ride that's built only for show. It looks good, performs well, and will earn some trophies.

Show Truck

Many of the vehicles at events such as the SEMA Show are show trucks. They're built primarily to display across the country. Sometimes they're put on jack stands to show their fully chromed undercarriages, and sometimes the truck has a motor but it may not be wired or run. They look pretty, but you wouldn't want to drive one to the store for fear of scratching the paint.

Planning

There's no reason why you can't have an overall goal and then pass milestones along the way.

Maybe you want to build a truck that will be featured on the cover of a magazine. If you want to body drop it, install air ride suspension, and give it a wild paint job with an interior to match, that requires a lot of time and money. So, lay it out as follows:

- Lower the truck with bolt-on modifications (bolt-on custom)
- Perform an engine swap with bolt-on modifications
- Complete a full paint job (moving toward being a mild custom)
- Upgrade the interior and stereo
- Add graphics (moving toward being a full custom)
- Magazine cover/Best of Show winner

The idea is to have something that you'll be able to use along the way—as long as things are progressing toward the goal. After all, if you buy all of the parts to lower the truck, most of them won't go to waste. Those dropped spindles will still be in play with the airbags. The coils and leaf-spring mounts probably won't be used at that point, but they can be resold. Swapping the engine can be completed in a week or two (depending on the type of upgrade), and you will still have something that is fun to drive.

Take the time to figure all of this out before you find a project truck. In the long run, you will save time and money, which are both invaluable.

As for this book, the aim is to shoot somewhere in the middle. Mild- and full-custom trucks are relatively attainable for the average builder and, frankly, the most fun to own. However, there is still a lot of good information available for show truck builders.

Silverado versus Cheyenne or W/T

Today, 25-plus years after these trucks left the showroom floor, there are still many options on the market. However, when it comes time to buy a project truck, the big choice still comes down to buying one that's stripped down or one with all of the options. Let's break it down.

The work truck (W/T) and Cheyenne models are pretty basic. They have vinyl-covered floors, bench seats, and manual windows. Silverados have all of the bells and whistles. Is it worth the extra cost? Well, it depends on the build.

Some show truck builders buy a cab and make everything work, including custom dashboards, fiberglass center consoles, and new bucket seats. If you go that route, it really doesn't matter what kind of truck is purchased because it will all be replaced. Who cares if there is a bench seat if you plan to install a set of Recaro seats anyway?

Conversely, if you desire a restoration or to build a period-correct sport truck in the vein of what was popular in the 1990s, all of those creature comforts are probably wanted.

Usually, the big deciding factor is the engine. Most W/T and Cheyenne models had either the 4.3L V-6 or the 305 V-8. If the engine will be replaced with an LS or LT (or even a Vortec V-8), it doesn't matter what's in the

This beautiful Chevy has graphics, a body drop, and large wheels. You could probably cruise it to the show instead of trailering it, which makes it a full custom. (Photo Courtesy Switch Suspension)

truck that you buy. However, if you don't plan to swap the engine, this might be a deal-breaker.

In all fairness, it's difficult to tell the difference between a 305 and a 350 when at a show, so that particular problem may not be a big deal. You may care more about gas mileage, which is what some people claim as their logic for owning the smaller V-8. However, the difference between a V-6 and V-8 is visually obvious, and while the V-6 is a reliable motor, it's not the one of choice for many connoisseurs.

The point of this is to look at the big picture. Consider what you're building, how you want to build it, and what's required to move forward. Then, base your purchase on that information.

Body and Drivetrain

Many different trucks can be found, and just as many different types of engines can be found. When it comes time to select the right truck, the engine choice is critical, particularly if the original will be kept in place. So, what do you need to look for? Well, let's begin by examining the options for a stock truck.

The base-model engine in these trucks is the 4.3L V-6. As the old adage goes, it's basically a 350-ci engine with two of the cylinders lopped off. However, that also means that it's a relatively torquey motor, and although it may not be the ideal engine, it can be tweaked and tuned to produce decent power numbers. Believe it or not, some people prefer the 4.3L because they want to install a twin-turbo setup under the hood—to each their own.

The next option was a 5.0L V-8. It was 305 ci, and it produced slightly better gas mileage than its larger cousin. It isn't a bad motor per se, but it's not as popular as the 350. The 305 is found on earlier models, and it was replaced by the Vortec 5000, which is also a 305.

The 5.7L V-8 is the engine that many people want, and it's fairly common. It's the classic 350-ci motor that Chevy produced for many years, and earlier models had a throttle-body injection (TBI) setup. Later, the Vortec 5700 V-8 replaced the traditional 350 engine, adding more horsepower and torque to the mix.

Finally, there is the 454. This is the 7.4L motor that came specifically in the 454 SS, a limited-edition model that was only produced for a few years. These engines can be found in some 2500 and 3500 trucks as well, which means that they can be swapped into a standard cab. These big-block V-8s are heavy and don't produce much horsepower, but they sound mean with a supercharger.

Now, these are the kinds of engines that should be found in a stock truck. However, that doesn't limit your options. For example, it is possible to purchase a V-6-equipped extra cab to save some cash, knowing that you have an LS swap that is ready to go. The same applies to any engine in this list. The fact is that you may buy a truck with the intent of changing the engine even if what's in there

This truck features the Vortec V-8 that was installed in OBS trucks of later years. It's reliable, and this particular one has been driven more than 240,000 miles.

This 454 V-8 is in a 1992 crew-cab dually. It's not as quick of a motor in this particular body, but it can scoot in a standard cab.

is doing just fine. As is a theme in this book, the choice is yours.

Fleetside versus Sportside

Craigslist, OfferUp, and Facebook Marketplace provide many options for a potential project vehicle, including the bed. There are two options: fleetside (then called wideside) and sportside (also known as stepside). The terms sportside and stepside are used interchangeably. Each one has its own pros and cons. Before going through the differences, I'll provide some historical context.

Most early trucks of the 1930s and 1940s came with a stepside bed. The idea was that if something was needed out of the back of the truck, there would be a way to lift yourself high enough to reach it. These trucks were extremely popular, and it wasn't until the 1950s that Chevrolet even offered a fleetside model. When the C10 era began, every truck had a stepside version, but the bed stayed virtually the same through 1987. That's 27 years of trucks with a bed that was very similar. Different, yes, but not much, particularly to the untrained eye. It wasn't until the introduction of the sportside in 1988 that things truly changed.

A 1988–1998 fleetside bed is made of 100-percent steel. So, whether you're tossing cement blocks into the bed or just cruising in it every day, it's metal, which is known to handle abuse. Sportside beds have a steel box, but the outside of the bed is made of fiberglass. At the time, that was new for General Motors. It was able to integrate the fenders into the bed sides in a cleaner way, and it looked much better than previous models.

What does all of this mean when buying a truck? It depends on how extreme you want to go. Many things can be done to a sportside bed to make it stand out. JDS Customs makes a set of billet step pads for $400, as does LG Billet for $575. Both are a classic style that have been around since the 1990s. Roll pans can also be purchased, but they're more difficult to find. It is necessary to fiberglass them in to look best, but it's doable.

Then, there's body drops. To body drop a sportside, the argument could be made that it's an easier process. Remove the bed sides, cut the bed floor, weld it up, and it's done. However, if you're running big wheels, the fenders get in the way. It is possible to raise them up and re-fiberglass the gap, but it doesn't look as good most of the time.

Fleetside beds are the most common (by far), so it may not be an issue in your search. There is the option to buy a fleetside and swap the bed later (and vice versa). But keep the pros and cons in mind when project shopping, and it'll make your build easier.

Extra Cab, Standard Cab, or Crew Cab

Cab size is another item to consider, and many factors are involved.

You are the first factor. Are you a tall person? Those who are 6 feet, 2 inches tall fit just fine in a standard cab. If you're someone who likes to stretch out a little, or you're taller, an extra cab or crew cab may be worth considering.

Extra cabs of later years have a third door, which makes it more convenient to get passengers in and out of the vehicle. While it doesn't make a ton of sense, it seems like most extra cabs sell for less money than the standard cabs. To save some money or to have the extra cabin space for speakers or the like, this may be a good option.

Crew cabs in 1/2-ton trucks are rare, but if a Centurion can be found and you want to carry people with you, go for it. Alternatively, buy a 3/4- or 1-ton crew cab and build a new chassis for it. That will be expensive, but it's arguably the best way to get a 1/2-ton crew cab built without hunting across the country.

Long-Bed versus Short-Bed

If this book was about 1967–1972 Chevys, or maybe even 1973–1987 Chevys, you might not have much of a choice. Even though they made short-bed trucks back then, they

While stepside trucks aren't as popular as fleetside trucks, the stepside trucks look good when they're modified.

fetch a pretty penny today, so many people buy a long-bed truck and cut them down.

With these trucks, that's not as much of an issue. No matter how many sellers on Craigslist and OfferUp say that these are getting difficult to find, they're just not. At the time that this book was written, a short-bed Silverado could be found for about $5,000, and a Cheyenne could be found for about $3,500.

Now, that assumes that a short-bed is wanted, which is not a big stretch. The shorter look is popular, but some people prefer some of the odder options. An article was published in *Street Trucks* about a man who wanted his unicorn truck: an extra-cab, long-bed Silverado. He bought it, built it, and it was killer. However, he was definitely in the minority.

Long-bed trucks are cheaper. There are a few reasons why, most of which should be fairly obvious. They're more common, so there's less demand. They're usually pretty beaten up, as long-beds were often used as work trucks and short-beds were often used as daily drivers. Since long-beds are just not as nice, they can be bought for a song. That doesn't mean they have to be kept as is, though.

Another option is to buy a long-bed truck and shorten it. This is popular with Chevy trucks of previous generations, but it's not as popular with the OBS. To shorten the bed requires shortening the frame and either cutting down the original bed or buying a new one. In both scenarios, some welding is required.

Of course, you could also go the other way and lengthen the frame to put a larger cab on the chassis. If a crew cab is purchased separately, the frame could be lengthened to fit the cab and then the shorter bed could be installed or the longer bed could be kept.

There are many different ways to go forward. It all depends on your confidence in modifying a truck, so take that for what it is.

This decision is up to you. Keep in mind that long-bed trucks are cheaper and potentially easier to find.

2WD versus 4WD

This book focuses primarily on two-wheel-drive trucks (2WD) and customizing them. However, I would be remiss to not mention the popularity of the four-wheel-drive (4WD) models, as that is very much a thing in the custom world.

For the uninitiated, the number in 2WD and 4WD refers to the number of active drive wheels available to the vehicle at any one time. Two-wheel-drive trucks put power down only to the rear two wheels via the axle. The output of four-wheel-drive trucks is primarily through the rear axle, but when the truck is put into either four-low or four-high, it can also drive the front wheels via a transfer case and drive axles.

Four-wheel-drive trucks have a few advantages. If the truck has

Extra-cab trucks aren't as popular with customizers, so they can usually be found for a more inexpensive price than the rest. If you're looking for a deal, this might be a good option.

The torsion bar is visible on the upper right side. It's connected to the lower control arm and comes toward the viewer. (Photo Courtesy Lonnie Thompson)

been lifted, you can do some fun off-road shenanigans. In addition, it's easier to get out of a sticky situation because the truck can be pulled as well as pushed out, depending on what gear is chosen. Basically, these trucks are designed to drive on-road and off-road, and it's up to you which path to choose.

Two-wheel-drive trucks can go off-road too. However, they don't have the added capability of the extra two drive wheels. The pre-runner industry is predicated on the off-road ability of 2WD trucks, so not having access to another pair of drive wheels is not necessarily a bad thing. Plenty of OBS trucks can be seen blasting across the desert using only their rear wheels for forward propulsion. If you're customizing a 2WD truck, most people prefer to lower them, and their suspension accommodates that quite nicely. Lowering a four-wheel-drive truck isn't quite as fun.

A 4WD truck has a similar yet different suspension setup in the front. There are still the control arms and tie-rods that are found in a 2WD model (Chevy moved away from solid axles up front with this generation). However, instead of springs, it has torsion bars. These run from the lower control arm to the frame, and they support the weight of the vehicle, just like a coil spring. They have a drive axle connecting the transmission to the front wheels, so the spindles are different too.

A 4WD truck can also be lowered. Some argue that it's better for autocrossing, as it's similar to an all-wheel-drive system but very different. However, it's much more difficult to do than one would think, and it is generally not worth the hassle.

One of your first decisions should be whether you want a two- or four-wheel-drive truck. If four is chosen, then lowering it won't be the most enjoyable process. Lifting it is significantly easier, but that's a topic for another book.

Renderings

Once you have an idea of what kind of truck you want to build, consider getting a rendering. You've probably seen one before. It is a mockup of a vehicle in its future state. Sometimes they're done by automotive manufacturers to show what next year's model will look like. However, in this case, it's all about your truck.

There are a few reasons to get a rendering. First, having a piece of art of your truck is a nice little keepsake. It's also aspirational. It shows what your truck will be if you keep moving forward. The rendering helps to cement your ideas and decide if they'll actually look good too.

You'll have cool ideas before and during the process. Some of them may be awesome, while others may be, well, bad. Or, once you see them, you realize that they're exactly what was done to someone else's truck years ago.

Those who create renderings can be found in many places. For example, check Instagram, where many artists are hocking their wares. In addition, magazines, such as *Street Trucks*, have many renderings. Just look for where the artist is given credit.

Getting a rendering is optional, but it's good to see your ideas come to life. In addition, it can provide motivation for you to make it happen.

SUVs

While this book is primarily about trucks, this particular era also had its fair share of SUVs, including the Suburban and Tahoe. The Tahoe was available in two- or four-door trim. These SUVs can be found for inexpensive prices too. Well, that's the case for most of them.

Let's take a moment to break this down. The rarest of these SUVs

This particular four-door Tahoe looks good when laid out on big billets. (Photo Courtesy Switch Suspension)

is the two-door, 2WD Tahoe, which was discussed in chapter 1. These SUVs are shorter than a standard-cab, short-bed pickup and look amazing when they are built correctly. Because of their rarity, they're often pretty pricey. For one with relatively low miles, expect to pay about $15,000. The exact same truck in 4WD goes for $5,000 to $8,000.

Similar things happen with the four-door Tahoe and Suburban. In some cases, these are $500 specials, but really, they don't get to be too expensive. At most, these things sell for around $7,500—and even that's pretty rare. In many markets, a four-door Tahoe can often be purchased for less than half of that price.

Then, there are the outliers: GMC Denalis and Cadillac Escalades. They're pretty affordable too, albeit slightly more expensive. Some of them are even cheaper than the trucks.

So, why purchase something like this? Because they're the underdogs. They're the relatively unpopular trucks that not everyone wants. They're the grocery getters that look amazing when laid on the ground. Since not everyone builds one, they're in a more rarified air. There's nothing wrong with that.

Besides, have you ever seen a body-dropped Suburban? They're pretty amazing to see in person. Plus, all of these vehicles share parts. A Denali front clip can be put on a 1988 Silverado and vice versa. Use the center console from an Escalade on a Tahoe or install the GMC front grille onto a Suburban. While the suspensions aren't identical, there are workarounds for all of them to make life easier.

My point is that you shouldn't sleep on the SUV crowd. If you're having a difficult time finding the truck of your dreams, think about something different. Maybe it'll bring better luck.

Duallies

Duallies are great. These are the huge (typically crew cab) trucks that have four wheels in the back and extended fiberglass fenders. They come with a 454-ci V-8 or a diesel engine, and they are designed for towing. In addition, they look killer when they are laid out on the ground.

For years, the big problem with duallies was the wheels. They couldn't be found with a decent design with a large enough diameter. Sure, it was possible to get 16-inch Neepers (a brand of wheel that was popular in the 1990s) in 1998. However, anything bigger was pushing the limit, and 16s were already out of style.

The change came when people started installing 19- and 22-inch wheels on their duallies, and when 24s became available, it was a wrap.

Popularity

So, why are duallies so popular, particularly among OBS fans? Well, the previous generation had duallies, and sure, they look pretty good laid out. However, 1992–2000 Chevy and GMC 3500s are unique. They have fiberglass fenders, which lend themselves to modification if there is a need to go lower. The previous generation used steel, and the next generation used plastic, which cracked easily. So, there are some inherent structural advantages with fiberglass as well. These fiberglass fenders bolt on and off, which means that if they need to be modified, it is not necessary to redo the entire bed—just the fenders.

Duallies come in all shapes and sizes, but they can be fairly easily found in crew cabs. Other than the super-rare Centurion (which is a crew-cab, short-bed truck), a crew-cab Chevy isn't an option unless you have a 3/4- or 1-ton truck. The coolest of those two choices is a dually.

Then, there's another aspect, which is the length. Duallies are often found in crew-cab, long-bed form. This makes for a monstrously long truck for sure. However, that also provides an abundance of space for passengers, which is important.

One of the main motivations just comes down to masculinity and

People love these trucks. (Photo Courtesy Ruben Castañon)

These are all crew-cab duallies, and there's not a single extra cab or standard cab in the bunch. That's likely what you'll find for sale too. (Photo Courtesy Ruben Castañon)

nostalgia. There's nothing more macho than a truck that can pull a house off its foundation, and there's something cool about a long truck with six big wheels laid out with a huge boat on its fifth-wheel hitch. There's also something to be said about how most men played with toy trucks as a kid. If you had a mini Peterbilt in your bedroom, a real-life dually is the next best thing that doesn't require a commercial driver's license (CDL).

Another nice bonus with the OBS dually is towing power. A custom truck guy is used to hearing people say that he ruined the truck by lowering it. Today, there are body dropped and bagged duallies that are pulling fifth-wheel trailers across the country, so there's nothing really ruined by modifying a truck. In addition, that also means taking a pair of Jet Skis to the lake on the weekend is no big deal.

Basically, if a dually is the goal, things need to be done slightly differently. All of the parts need to be beefier because they are pulling more weight for the truck and whatever is being towed. Although a lower profile tire can be used, it can't be too low, otherwise you lose towing capacity. In addition, things are going to be expensive because there's a lot of truck to build.

With all of that being said, building or owning a dually is on the bucket list for many people. It is also a great option for someone starting out.

At the end of the day, these trucks are just cool. There's nothing quite like seeing a long and low dually pull up and lay itself out on some 22-inch wheels. Is a dually for you? The rest of the market sure seems to like these trucks.

This Centurion dually short-bed may make you do a double take because most duallies are much longer. (Photo Courtesy Ruben Castañon)

Look how close the fenders are to the taillights. (Photo Courtesy Ruben Castañon)

The Rare Dually Short-Bed

Let's do a quick refresher on the Centurion OBS. In the late 1990s, a conversion van company named Centurion created 1/2-ton, crew-cab, short-bed trucks using only General Motors parts. Centurion did this in 2WD and 4WD variations, as well as 3/4- and 1-tons. However, what was done to the heavier-duty models was slightly different.

A 3/4- or 1-ton crew cab could often be bought off the dealership floor, but it came with a long bed. However, in the late 1990s, Centurion offered a setup with a short bed. If the 1/2-ton, 2WD version is rare, the short-bed dually is even more so. There are very few of them on the road, but when they're customized, they look amazing.

You could always build your own. It would involve shortening the frame, potentially tweaking the gas tank situation, and doing some custom work. However, if you own this book, you're probably okay with that.

Semitruck Wheels

In the 1990s, when the OBS dually scene was just starting to go nuts, there weren't a lot of options for wheels. Back then, the best option was a set of 16s with some monster tires, and it didn't really match up with the trend of going to larger wheel diameters. By the time that regular full-size trucks had 20-inch wheels, the 16s on a dually looked small. It was time for a change.

The next best option was to use a wheel from a semitruck (with adapters). However, these were 22.5 inches (not 22 inches). To make them work took some machining magic. However, that's exactly what some people did, and at first, it wasn't all great.

One complicating factor was the width of the semi wheel. In the back, four wheels are needed to be a true dually, but getting them to tuck under the fenders could require narrowing the axle. This added to the overall expense of the project. In addition, these wheels were expensive. Some owners decided to just buy four, and then they'd run a smaller-diameter inner wheel and tire combination that could not only support the truck but also save them some cash.

Another problem was the wheel itself. People would buy used semi wheels because they were substantially cheaper, but some of those wheels may have seen abuse. They could even be out of round.

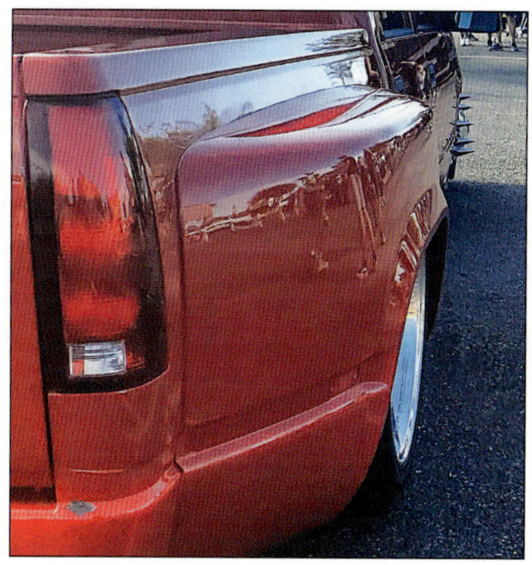

After Castañon had the truck bagged by Lowboy Motorsports, the axle was narrowed, providing the space to tuck the rims. (Photo Courtesy Ruben Castañon)

This truck (circa late 2008) featured 19-inch semitruck wheels. This was common at the time and is still in style.

Before his truck was bagged, Ruben Castañon's rear wheels stuck outside of the fenders. (Photo Courtesy Ruben Castañon)

However, new semi wheels (often referred to as "semis" in the scene) were okay. People even began machining their own patterns into them to create their own one-off designs, and that was cool too.

Today, dually owners have an abundance of options. Lowboy Motorsports, a custom shop in Mesa, Arizona, offers several wheel options. It is even possible to get wheels that don't require narrowing the axle. Whether you want something that is one-off or just a basic deal, Lowboy Motorsports knows how to get things done correctly because the company has been working on these trucks for decades.

Potential Issues

One thing to think about when working on the suspension of a dually is the combination of the wheels and the fenders, specifically the rears. The rear fenders on a dually bolt onto the bed, and they are made of fiberglass. This works to your advantage and disadvantage. On the plus side, if they need to be cut for any reason, that can be done and the gaps can be filled with fiberglass. It's a relatively easy modification, and it doesn't require a welder. On the downside, fiberglass is not as strong as steel, so it can chip if it is dragged down the road when it is laid out, specifically if it is body dropped.

So, why should you modify the rear fenders? There are two primary reasons.

First, they need to be modified if the wheels are too wide for the body. Some people purchase dually wheels with a very deep dish because it looks cool. However, the only way to fit them under the stock fenders is to narrow the axle, which is not an inexpensive process.

Instead, the fenders can be widened. This also usually means lengthening them, as they have a taper built into the design. This creates a very large fender.

Second, if the plan is to body drop the truck, or even just run larger-diameter wheels and tires, the stock outer fenders may not work. It is possible to run 22-inch wheels with a smaller-diameter tire on the rear without modifying the fenders. However, anything larger requires cuts to provide clearance at the top of the fender. The solution for many people is to section the panel.

Sectioning the panel requires cutting the fender lengthwise down the middle, raising the top portion, and then filling in the gap with fiberglass. Again, it's doable, but the fender ends up running over the stock bodyline. Not many people integrate that detail into their dually fenders, and that means they can look a little bit odd. The proportioning can also seem weird, and if you section and widen your fenders, that's quite the difference.

Now, you dont have to do any of this. You can lay your dually out on bags and 22s without cutting the fenders at all. However, if the goal is to body drop the truck or use larger wheels, look out for those other potential problems.

Towing

Duallies were made for towing, and that doesn't change much once

This dually has a smooth roll pan with the license plate that's hidden somewhere else.

This shows the frame-mounted tow hitch. This particular truck has a bridge notch and airbags, but the owner doesn't plan to pull a fifth-wheel. This way, the truck can still tow, but it's not as obvious on a daily basis.

alterations are made to the truck. However, it does matter how those modifications are made and what kind of towing will be done.

The first and simplest thing to think about is an overload airbag setup. If the dually is lowered, towing a trailer may cause the frame to bottom out on the axle. If that's the case, an overload setup is a pretty simple fix. It bolts in place and acts as additional support for the suspension. If you're going to pull a trailer, air up the bags and get going. It won't bottom out, and the ride will improve. Look up "helper bags," online and you'll get the same result.

Next, consider how the modifications are made. The big issue here is the frame. If you make a C-notch in the back, make sure that thing is super strong. Dually frames are larger than 1/2-ton models, and that means the notch is going to be sized appropriately. Cutting away too much material without reinforcing it properly creates a weak point at that notch. If there is a frame-mounted hitch behind the notch, that weak point could be disastrous. Make sure that the notch is made correctly.

Of course, another option is a bridge notch, which is what a lot of people who tow with duallies use, even if they don't want an adjustable suspension. The bridge notch gives them the ability to easily do a fifth-wheel mount, and that's awesome for towing. It's also stronger than a bolt-in C-notch.

Airbag mounts can be created too. Why use airbags if you don't want an adjustable suspension? As helper bags, of course. This method produces a fifth-wheel mount, air assist for loads, and a stronger frame. It's a win-win-win.

Rust

No matter where you live, there is the potential to uncover rust at some point in the build. Even trucks that were "true Southern California barn finds" may have spent some time in upstate New York, leaving enough salt to cause their rockers to age prematurely. Some rust can be handled during repair, but there's no reason to give yourself more work.

Before paying for your next project, go over it with a fine-tooth comb. Look for the tell-tale signs of rust: bubbling under the paint, holes in panels, or actual rust that's peeking through the finish. Remember, if there is a little rust, there's always more to be found.

The common areas that rust out on this truck are the cab corners and rockers (like pretty much every GM truck). Replacement panels can be found fairly easily at places such as LMC Trucks. It is also possible to fabricate your own. Another option is to patch the piece and not replace the entire panel, assuming that it's not too far gone.

The fenders are usually okay, but it depends on where the truck spent most of its life. Check for damage under the battery tray on the passenger's side as well as the area under the hood by the latch. The cowl can also

Peeling paint such as this is common. General Motors had some issues with sealer and basecoat compatibility in the 1990s, and sometimes results such as this were produced. (Photo Courtesy Lonnie Thompson)

The frame might get some rust on it too. Keep an eye out for that. (Photo Courtesy Lonnie Thompson)

have issues, particularly if foliage and the like gets behind the plastic and rots.

In the back of the truck, the presence of rust depends on the type of bed. Fleetside beds are metal, so there may be rust in the corners, around the fenders, and on the tailgate. Sportside beds only have that problem with the tailgate for the most part (they're primarily made of fiberglass), but check the floor as well.

Rust isn't something to fear, but it is something to prepare to fix. Think about it before buying, and you'll be ahead of the game.

Bargains and Parts Trucks

There are several different ways to build a truck, but it generally falls into one of two categories: buy a really clean truck and customize it or pick up a bucket for an inexpensive price and fix it along the way.

Let's take a moment to talk about the bargain trucks. These trucks may only need paint, the interior may be moldy, or the engine may have a hole in it that is the size of your fist. Whatever the issue is, the truck is affordable because it needs a lot of work. That's definitely appealing, because truck builds aren't cheap. Saving some money on the front end can certainly work to your advantage.

However, here's the thing: bargains are only cheap up front. More often than not, you'll end up spending more in the long term.

Why? The biggest reason is time. It is time-consuming to look for the parts that are missing. Unless you know these trucks really well, you may not even know that a part is gone until it is needed. A bargain truck will nickel and dime you through the whole process. The one way that it may work to your advantage is if you realize the truck is just too far gone to be your main build. Then, you find yourself a truck that does have what you need: a parts truck.

A parts truck is pretty much what it sounds like. It may not have a bed, the front may have been wrecked, and it may have a salvage title or no title at all. Whatever the deal is, the truck is inexpensive enough that a junkyard would buy it.

Now, you have parts for your build, and buying a truck was probably less expensive than buying the parts by themselves. These trucks aren't always inexpensive, but deals can occasionally be found, which may make it worth it. You will need to find a place for the parts truck as well as a nearby junkyard or someone to buy the leftover components. That way, you recoup some of your investment.

If items are needed for your project and they can't be found at a local junkyard or through an online seller, consider buying a parts truck.

These seats were pulled from a parts truck. At a junkyard, this may have cost a few hundred dollars, but the entire truck may only cost slightly more.

This hood came from the same truck, as did the grille in the background. The bed wasn't in great shape, but buying a parts truck allows you to save a significant amount of money overall.

Consider an SUV

If you're looking for a parts truck, consider a Suburban, a Tahoe, a Denali, or an Escalade. Looking at the SUVs from the doors forward, they have most of the same parts (with a few exceptions). The doors are the same, the front ends are mostly the same, and the interior will also bolt up.

So, why should these models be considered? Because often it's difficult to find a short-bed truck with everything that you want that's not pricey. These vehicles were used by landscapers, construction workers, etc., so some are beat up. However, the SUVs were owned mostly by suburban moms and the like, so they're often in much better shape (relatively). In addition, because they're not quite as popular today, they're often cheaper too. In addition, they were built until 2000, so you can extend your year search out a little bit further.

Your smartphone may have some cool tricks up its sleeve. In this case, it was used to measure the distance between mounting locations. Then, a screenshot was taken for reference.

From an interior perspective, there are a few other bonuses. Many of the SUVs came with bucket seats, which may not be the case on a truck. That also means they have a center console, which is most likely on your potential wish list. Diving into the Denali and Escalade lineup also means different kinds of consoles that waterfall from the dash, which may or may not be your style.

If the goal is to change the look of your truck, the Denali and Escalade are great choices. The front ends on both were very popular conversions for a while, and there are still devotees of the look today. The interior is also a bit more refined, with woodgrain trim on the doors and leather. If you find either a Denali or an Escalade for an inexpensive price (or find one at a wrecking yard), that find could result in an upgrade to your interior for an inexpensive price.

Don't restrict yourself to the standard Chevy and GMC trucks. Start looking at SUVs too. ■

This isn't a pretty picture, but it shows what it looks like when you're hunting for a center console and need to know how it fits. In this case, this is inside of a Tahoe.

What You Know and What You Don't

So far, you've read about all of the different types of 1988–1998 GM trucks, what can be done to them, and how to make the right decision. However, there's one part that hasn't been tackled yet: you. That's because you are an important element of this entire build. If you're going to be involved in any way other than opening your checkbook and paying a bunch of shops to do the work, you need to know what you know and what you don't. That will help determine what you can do on your own and what needs to be farmed out.

Think first about what you know. If you've done a lot of suspension work, great. That aspect of the build is covered. Many people know how to wrap interior panels, and if you're one of them, you can use that to your advantage. Maybe you've painted a motorcycle or two, and stepping up to a truck seems logical. Lean on your skill set and know that will be one of your strengths for this build.

Then, think about what you don't know. Have you ever rebuilt an engine? If not, that's something to take to an expert. How about paint? If you don't have the know-how or location to spray the truck, then it's probably best to leave that to the experts. The same goes with interiors, suspension, and everything else. If you're not an expert or you're concerned that you're going to do more harm than good, consider farming it out.

Go through this book and look at each chapter. If you think you can do those things, great. If not, find a shop that can and make sure that you can afford their prices.

With all of that being said, don't sell yourself short. You *can* do all of this stuff yourself. It's going to take time and money, but what's the worst thing that could happen? You'd have to spend more time and more money to fix it? Sure, that's not great. However, what if you did a good job? Now, you have a new skill to add to your resume and you saved yourself money in the process. Isn't that a good thing?

Selecting a Truck Based on Your Skill Set

Now that you're thinking about what you can and can't do, apply that to the trucks you're potentially buying.

For example, say that you're an ex-painter and you know how to make a truck straight as an arrow. You've also worked with interiors here and there, so you feel pretty good about that, and you're comfortable enough with suspensions to do the 4/6 drop that you planned. So, what kind of truck do you get?

In this scenario, a truck with the clear coat peeling and a driver's seat that's shot would be right up your alley. It's a good price because it's not very appealing to other people, but for you, it's perfect.

Now, lets say that you're an engine guy. You have at least 10 builds under your belt and you know exactly what your next truck is going to have: an LSX. You have experience with suspensions, but you have no experience with painting. Fortunately, you have a guy for that. Unfortunately, he's expensive.

In this situation, the right truck might have a V-6. If the paint is good and the interior is fine, the engine doesn't matter. After all, you're planning to replace it anyway. As long as the paint and bodywork doesn't look like it'll be too expensive, you're good.

Run through scenarios like this with your own situation and potential projects. Determining what you know and what you don't and then applying it to the truck you want will result in a project that's rarer than the rest: one that gets done. At the end of the day, that is the best kind of project.

If you're an expert fabricator, such as the folks at Grunion Customs in Phoenix, Arizona, then this won't intimidate you.

CHAPTER 3

Teardown and Organization

So, you bought a truck? Good job. Now, it's time to tear it down to the frame to build the truck of your dreams.

Of course, if this is your first time doing it, you're probably not sure where to begin. Don't worry, it can be done. Start with some basic organizational ideas and move forward from there.

Teardown

While disassembling a truck may seem straightforward, that's not the case. There is often months or years between disassembly and reassembly, and sometimes someone else is doing some of the reassembly. It can be a real problem.

The solution is to be organized, specifically during the teardown process. Here are some guidelines:

1. **If the bolt can be put back in its place, do so.**
   For example, if you're removing the headers from the engine, loosely thread the bolts back into place (after the heavy lifting). Do this in every situation.
   Why? Many other bolts will look similar. It will be difficult to determine which one goes where during reassembly. By not relying on memory, you're making your future self more efficient, which increases productivity.
2. **If the bolt can't be put back in its place, make sure that it's labeled and in a container.**
   Not every bolt can go back where it started. If that's the case, put it in a bag. Use resealable sandwich bags and label them with a permanent marker. It isn't necessary to have a bag for every bolt, but make sure to keep them organized to avoid future confusion.
3. **Categorize the parts and keep them separated.**
   All of the engine parts should be clearly marked and in one place. All of the transmission parts should be clearly marked and in a different place. At no point should the engine and transmission parts mix. As the song "Come out and Play" by the Offspring says, "You gotta keep 'em separated."

If you don't obey the guidelines above, you won't remember where everything goes during reassembly. In addition, when you're working on a big truck, there are so many different parts to remember. However, if they are sorted by category (engine, transmission, interior, bed, etc.), at least you know where to start. Does that mean you're going to have a little parts shop in your workspace? Sure. In addition, this may take up more space than just dumping every bolt into a coffee can. However, the more time you take to organize parts at the beginning of the build, the less time you'll need to search for parts during reassembly.

Organization

There are many different types of parts (from big dashboards to little screws), and you'll need some way to organize all of them. There are many different ways, but there are a few methods that work really well.

For larger parts, buy some shelving. Large steel and wood units can be found at the local home center, and they work really well and are affordable. Look for models that will hold fenders, door panels, dashboards, and all of the other awkward parts that don't necessarily fit anywhere else. If you can put your seats on the top shelf, that works too. Basically, anything that can't easily fit into a box should be stored on the shelving.

For middle-sized parts, such as alternators, speakers, steering wheels, etc., use boxes or plastic bins. Cardboard boxes are great because they're cheaper and can be reused later for shipping. However, some plastic bins are clear, which makes it easier to find parts later when necessary. Select whichever option works best for you and your budget.

Anything that fits into a plastic resealable bag comes next. This includes screws, spark-plug wires, fuse boxes, and any other components that you feel comfortable putting in a Ziploc bag and storing on a shelf or inside another box.

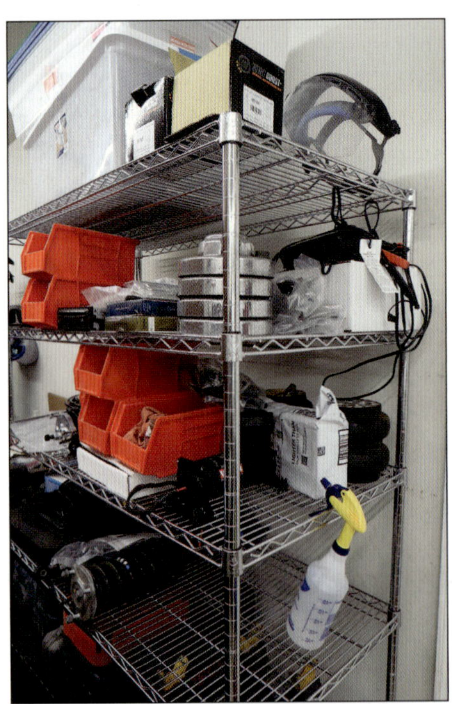

The top two shelves on this rolling rack hold parts for a 1998 Tahoe project, while the two shelves below hold parts for a car build. Organizing everything clearly helps significantly, particularly during reassembly.

Labeling

These boxes and containers aren't very useful if you don't know what is in them. That's why a system for labeling is important. When disassembling a truck, you can keep track of what bolt goes where and how many different ways a particular component fits. However, during reassembly six months later, it's easy to forget where everything goes. That's why there are a few things that are important to do if you want to keep your sanity.

First, use a permanent marker, such as a Sharpie, and label every box or container. Be as detailed as possible. For example, an alternator is pretty clearly an alternator. However, the driver-side door hinges may not be as obvious on first glance, and you don't want to mix them up. If necessary, use painter's tape to label which side is up. Use a twist-tie label on bigger parts if that'll refresh your memory. If it's in a bag, explain exactly what the bag contains in detail.

You can also go a step further, particularly with screws. Although a permanent marker can be used, the lettering will fade over time if the project takes years to finish. One solution is to use an index card. Use a pen to write a detailed description of the part inside. If it's a screw, explain exactly where it goes. For example, you might write, "Left front side of dash, under steering wheel, right of e-brake release." If it's a bolt, write down the size of the socket or wrench. Everything written on that card may seem like overkill, but when it comes time to put everything back into place, you'll know exactly where everything goes.

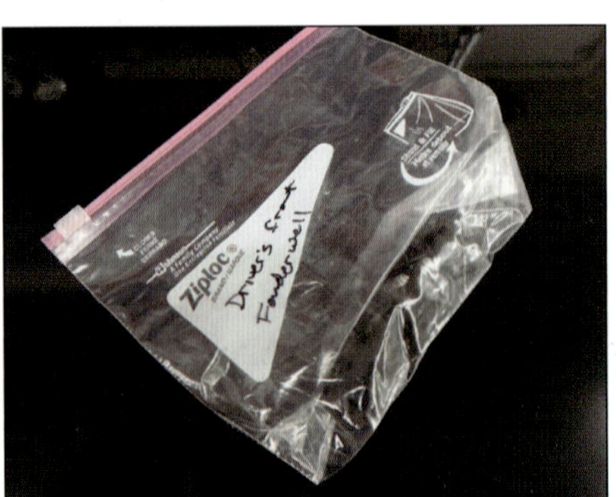

Resealable plastic bags are handy. Get the ones with the better zipper, such as this one. They stay tight longer, which means that the chance of losing parts that are stored in them is reduced.

Using a Notebook

A tip for first-time builders is to use a notebook. The ideal version is one that'll fit in your back pocket, but you can go bigger if your eyesight isn't what it used to be or you just prefer the larger format. The idea is to note anything that you might not remember later. It should be convenient enough to use anywhere, so having a hard cover is key. It should also have a place to hold a pen.

This notebook is from a company called Leuchtturm1917. It is available online at Leuchtturm1917.us. It also includes one of the company's pen loops. It is small enough to keep in your pocket while you work.

Say that you're tearing down a center console on a 1997 GMC, and there are a bunch of Torx bolts holding everything together. Your notebook could say, "T20 Upper lid + rear cupholder." You can fold up and place labels inside of the notebook if that helps or include phone numbers to local shops. Having all of these things in one place helps significantly. Don't forget to label the front of the notebook too.

Use a Camera

Cell phones with cameras are common. Taking photos and shooting videos of your project is not only good for your records but also for your memory.

Pick up a cheap tripod for $20. It doesn't need to be very tall, but it should stand up easily in the cab. When you're doing something that may require future reference, use the phone camera to capture a video.

A video can be helpful to document the process of removing the dashboard. It can be a frustrating process, and it seems like every truck is different. By filming the removal, you'll see (and hear) all of your frustrations and remember what to do (and what not to do) when it comes time to reassemble.

The same applies with photos. Take a photo every time that a bolt is removed to show where it goes. Document the length of the screw next to its location. Do whatever you think will help later.

It is helpful to print those photos and place them in the bags or boxes with the parts. So, if you lose the phone and/or images are lost, you're still covered. Alternatively, they can be saved to the cloud.

Basic Tools

To perform many of the tasks that are covered in this book, a collection of tools need to be used to cover the basics.

Basic socket and ratchet sets are needed (metric and standard deep-well and shallow-well sets). While this is an American truck, several metric bolts were involved in the assembly of these trucks, so have those on hand as well. Various lengths of extensions are helpful too.

Have 1/4-, 3/8-, and 1/2-inch-drive sockets and ratchets on hand. The ratchets should be long and short handled. While there aren't many situations where a 12-point socket is needed over a 6-point socket, know that there is a difference. A 6-point socket provides a more secure grip than a 12-point socket, but some bolts

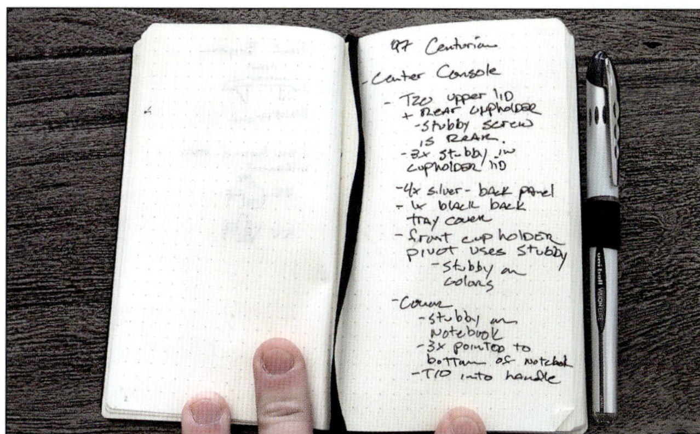

On the 1997 Centurion project, this page shows details regarding how to take apart the center console, while the previous page has a diagram. In addition, dot-grid or graph-paper notebooks are available.

This toolbox holds a complete set of wrenches and sockets in its drawers so that many of the tools you'll need are ready to go.

This mechanic's toolbox cost about $270 at Lowe's. It's a great way to keep tools on hand and nearby when working on a truck.

and nuts require a 12-point socket to fit correctly.

Click-type torque wrenches and sockets are critical, particularly when working on the engine. Everything on an engine should be torqued down properly, and while some people slam bolts on with an impact wrench and count the "oogah-doogahs," it's better to be more precise.

Standard and metric wrenches are another good purchase, and ratcheting wrenches are helpful. They cost more, but you'd be surprised how often you'll reach for a pair of those when working under the hood—or anywhere else.

While many mechanics have gone years without purchasing sets of standard and metric stubby wrenches, I suggest purchasing one early in the process. They're not extremely expensive (Lowe's sells the Craftsman version of each set for about $30), and they come in handy. There will be many occasions where it's necessary to crack off a nut but a ratchet or a traditional wrench won't fit.

Brake-line wrenches are specialty tools, but they're in this category because they're wrenches as well. Don't use a traditional wrench on a brake line because they can slip and round off the hex, creating major issues. Get them in standard and metric.

A hammer will be used more than you'd think. Get a dead-blow hammer. These help with tasks such as separating the ball joints. Just in case, also have a 5- or 10-pound sledgehammer handy to remove the nasty stuff.

Plastic panel tools are important when working on the interior. Many components are held in place with clips, and these tools not only avoid damaging the truck but they also make removing these panels significantly easier. If the truck has manual windows, make sure that the plastic panel tool kit includes one for those clips too.

Philips and flathead screwdrivers are required in varying lengths. A set of nut drivers may also come in handy, but they're not required. A ratchet (or ratchet and extension) can always be used.

A Torx bit set may be needed on occasion, but it's not very common on these trucks.

Safety Equipment

The correct safety equipment is required while you work. Otherwise, you risk injuring yourself—potentially permanently.

Begin with eye protection: goggles or an entire face shield—or both if you're feeling paranoid. This project requires using a grinder and other electric tools, and something can get into your eye if you don't wear eye

These wrench organizers by Ernst Manufacturing are magnetic, so they stick to the toolbox.

Safety glasses such as these are affordable. Cheap safety glasses are available for less than $5, or you can spend a little bit more for something such as this from Milwaukee. Protecting your eyes is important.

A face shield is to the left of two sets of headphones. Having these on hand is critical to avoid injury to your vision and hearing.

protection. You definitely want to avoid a trip to the emergency room.

Hearing protection comes in the form of over-the-ear muffs or foam ear plugs. Whichever type of hearing protection you choose, wear them when using loud equipment. Electric and pneumatic tools make a lot of noise, and extended periods of time at over 80 decibels can damage your hearing.

Basic clothing is also important. Welding while wearing shorts and flip flops is usually a bad idea. While it may be inconvenient to put on something that covers more of your skin, there is a reason that most professionals gear up. Long pants, work boots (preferably with a steel toe), and a long-sleeve shirt isn't always great in warm weather, but it will protect you from errant sparks, etc. In addition, consider a jumpsuit if you just want to have one outfit to wear in the garage. Wearing a shop apron is another option. Both provide additional protection and usually have several pockets too.

Have gloves on hand. A solid latex glove works well when dexterity is needed, such as when removing interior panels or reaching under a dash. They don't provide much protection, but they'll keep your hands clean. Use thicker mechanic's gloves when working on something that requires knuckle protection, such as when wrenching under the hood. If you do any welding, use the appropriate gloves. Tungsten inert gas (TIG) welding gloves are different than metal inert gas (MIG) welding gloves, so keep gloves on hand for whichever type of welding you do.

The only other thing to think about from a safety perspective is the shop itself. Clean as you work and get rid of frayed or cut extension cords. Not only will you be able to find your tools faster but you'll also reduce tripping hazards. To keep tools nearby, consider a mechanic's tool cart. These

Tool Quality

Some people are of the opinion that the cheapest tool they can get for the job is just fine. If it breaks, it's affordable enough to get a new one, so they might as well just do that. On the other hand, expensive tools usually have a warranty and should last a lifetime. So, which way do you go?

This is a heavily contested debate, but it ultimately comes down to your budget. It may not be possible to invest thousands into a tool collection, and that's fine. While you can just replace tools when they break, it sucks (and is inefficient) to have to stop what you're doing to go to the store to buy a replacement.

The general consensus around the internet is this: spend more on higher-quality tools that will be used often. This typically refers to sockets, ratchets, screwdrivers, and wrenches, but whatever you feel applies works as well. Then, you can buy cheaper single-use tools. So, if it breaks, it's not a big deal. It was used for what you needed, and the probability is low that it will ever be needed again.

This is your decision. So, give it some thought before spending money. ■

These gloves are available at Lowe's. They're more expensive than low-quality gloves, but they don't tear easily. The less-expensive gloves tend to rip.

Thicker gloves are best when you're worried about heat or you need additional protection. Mechanix gloves are the standard, but many other options are available.

usually hold all of the sockets and wrenches and can be wheeled easily around your garage.

Electric Tools

In the past, a full suite of pneumatic and corded electric tools was needed to work on a truck. Today, with the proliferation of battery-powered tools, almost anything can be done without a cord or air hose in the way.

While it is possible to buy tools from any company, it works best to stay within a particular system. If you do so, when a battery dies, it can be swapped out with a spare that's already charged and ready to go. It also allows you to reduce the number of chargers that are needed.

Many brands offer battery-powered tools, including Makita, Craftsman, DeWalt, Ryobi, Milwaukee, etc. To build a collection, find your favorite brand and go from there.

A reciprocating saw (also known as a Sawzall, which is what Milwaukee named its reciprocating saw) is a good tool to start with. An entire truck can be cut into tiny pieces with a good reciprocating saw and a few blades. On that same note, get blades that will cut through both thin and thick metal. Milwaukee's Torch lineup is great for hacking through a frame, and its multi-material blades work well for everything else.

Grinders (possibly two) are needed. Most of the time, a good 4½-inch model will get the job done. Although, the added horsepower and size of a 6-inch model might be preferred, particularly when grinding on the frame. The paddle-style models work best for smoothing out welds and are generally easier to maneuver.

Grinding discs are necessary as well. Get the flap-disc-style model in various grits as well as cutting discs and grinding discs. All of them will be used in various parts of the build. As a bonus, if you have two grinders, one can be loaded up with a flap disc and another with a grinding disc. That way, you can just swap between the two as you work, saving time in the process.

Angle grinders and die grinders are also very good to have. Using an angle grinder with a Roloc disc helps significantly when grinding down welds. Die grinders are extremely handy. Whether cutting out a panel or hacking through a rivet, a good die grinder with a cut-off wheel is great to have.

A drill is useful, particularly when it's cordless. Get one with a 1/2- or 3/8-inch chuck. A smaller

Milwaukee offers many battery-powered options, and they can be stored on these Packout wall kits. However, if you're not a fan of Milwaukee, many other choices are available.

This battery-powered impact wrench has a mar-free socket attached for removing lug nuts without scratching the rims.

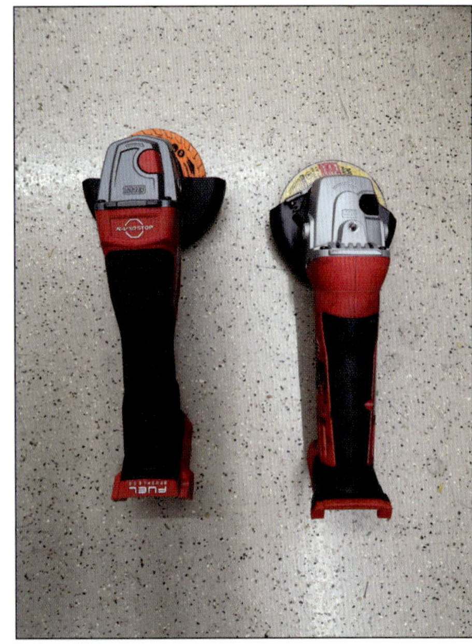

In this case, one grinder has a flap disc and the other has a cut-off wheel. Having both preloaded is nice and increases efficiency.

model designed just for installing and removing screws comes in handy when working on (and under) the dashboard.

Impact wrenches used to be pneumatic only, but if you have the cash, spring for an electric model. Milwaukee has one that automatically lowers its speed when the nut is freed, which makes it fantastic for use on wheels. There are also smaller angled impacts out there now for tighter jobs, and they are available in sizes smaller than 1/2 inch too.

Electric ratchets also used to be pneumatic only. Today, battery-powered 1/2-, 3/8-, and 1/4-inch models are available. These increase your efficiency during the tedious jobs. While a manual version is needed, particularly when it comes time to break some bolts free, they help you save your energy for the more strenuous jobs.

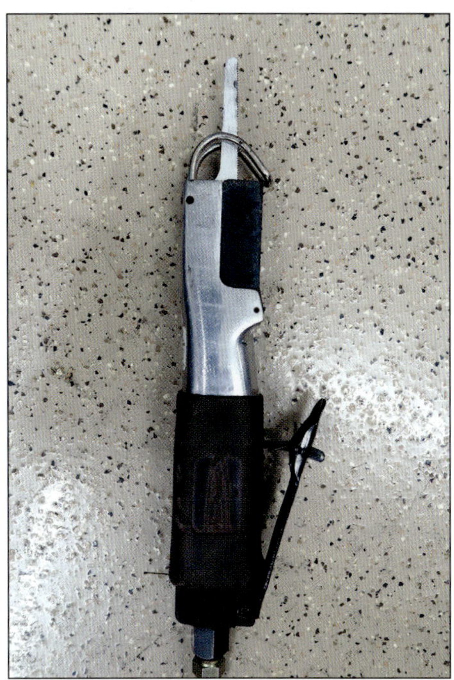

This tool gets jammed regularly, which can be frustrating, but all air saws can get jammed. With that being said, air saws can be used for very precise cuts, which is important in various situations.

Here's the workhorse: a pneumatic impact wrench. This works well not only with lug nuts but also for taking care of pesky, stuck bolts.

Pneumatic Tools

It's not necessary to buy as many pneumatic tools as you would have a decade ago, some are still useful. In fact, even if it's just for airing up the truck for the first time when installing airbags, having a good air compressor and tools is convenient.

Almost all of the tools listed in the electric section are available in pneumatic form as well. If you already have an air version and don't mind dealing with the hose, there's no reason to spend money on something new.

Regarding an air compressor, use something with a 200-psi max limit and a decent amount of storage. The idea is to have enough PSI available to be able to lift a heavy truck with airbags, while still being able to run air tools for a window of time. The more air storage you have, the longer these tools can be used before the tank needs to be refilled, so consider that when making the purchase.

A dual action (D/A) sander is good for doing bodywork, as are other pneumatic sanding tools. An air file comes in handy for larger panels.

Although electric saws are available, pneumatic air saws are typically smaller and easier to work with. They can jam up, and that gets frustrating, but they're able to cut tight radii without running into too many issues.

If cash is too tight to purchase an electric impact, that's okay. A pneumatic one will work just as well. Get a 1/2-inch model for heavy-duty jobs, such as wheels and suspension parts. A 3/8-inch version is also handy for smaller items.

Pneumatic grinders, including die grinders, work well as well too.

Note that some stores sell lower-quality items than others. When it comes to pneumatic tools, the lower-quality ones tend to leak. The air in the tank should be going into the equipment, not the atmosphere. So, invest in quality pneumatic tools whenever possible. No matter what you end up buying, lubricate air tools regularly so that they last longer.

Lifts and Jacks

You do not *need* a lift. People have been working on these trucks for years without lifts. However, having a lift certainly doesn't hurt.

A two-post lift can help with everything from simple tasks to back-breaking work. For example, use a lift to remove a truck bed. Just unbolt everything from the chassis and place the arms under the corners of the bed. Lift it up slowly, and you're done. The same applies for the cab, which is a huge advantage when doing a body drop or something similar.

Some homes are built with post-tension slabs, which means you can't drill into them blindly to install a traditional lift. Fortunately, a few options are available.

If you do want to bolt down a lift, find a local slab X-ray specialist. The specialist can scan a home's foundation and see where the tension cables sit so that you don't accidentally hit one during installation.

Alternatively, look at the mobile lifts on the market today. The Quick Jack is a relatively affordable option that works well for these trucks. It can handle the weight, and when you are done, just hang them on the wall. It really is that easy.

If you don't want a lift, no problem. Use a high-quality 2- or 3-ton jack. Look for a low-profile version if possible, particularly if you plan to lower the truck. Then, invest in decent jack stands. A few years ago, there was a recall on a popular store's jack stands because they were failing. Get good ones, because it's your life that you're putting on the line. Buy 8 to 12 of them. The more you have, the easier it is to get everything supported properly, particularly when working on the rear axle or notching the frame.

Specialty Tools

It is necessary to remove the truck's bed, and if you don't have a lift, another method is to use a hoist. There are many options here for under $300, but consider buying one that folds up. This can save a bit of space in the garage, while still giving you access to the tool.

Cab- and bed-lifting tools are available for hoists as well. These bolt in where the chain goes, or they hang from the chain itself. They have a central lifting point that is used to lift off the part. In the case of the bed, it lifts out similar to an engine. To remove the cab, the mount is on the top of the hoist, which makes it a bit trickier to finesse, but it can be done.

If you have an engine hoist, an engine stand and engine leveler is nice to use. The stand is great once the transmission has been separated from the engine and you want to install a new camshaft or just work on various parts. The leveler makes it a little bit easier to get the motor in and out of

Buy several jack stands. You really can't have too many of them, particularly with these trucks. Make sure that they're from a reputable brand because they will protect you from injury.

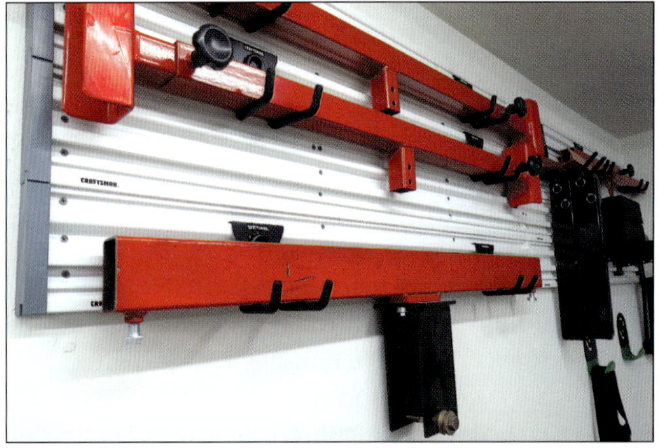

The red pieces on the wall are components for a cab-lifting kit and a bed-lifting kit, and both work with an engine hoist. They may not be used often, but if the goal is to get something done by yourself, they're indispensable.

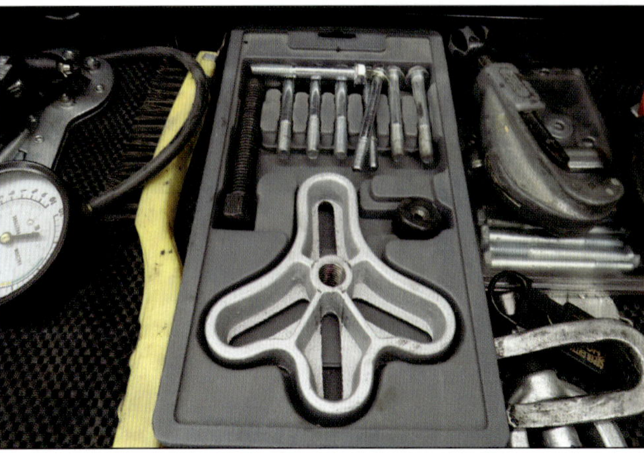

This is a steering-wheel-puller kit. It may not be needed often, but it will save you from frustration.

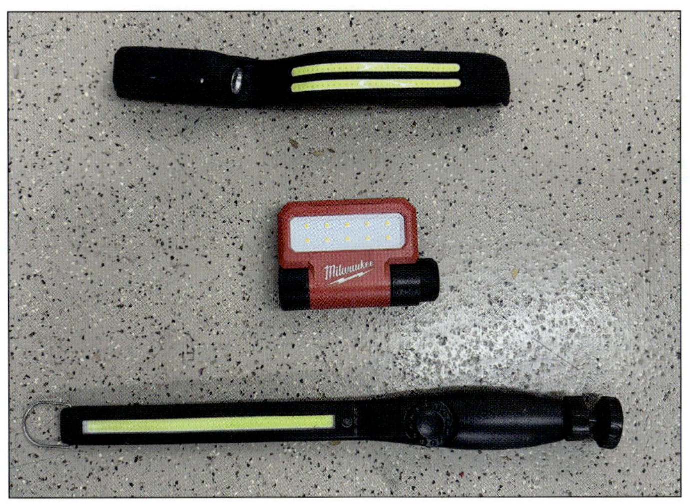

From top to bottom, this is a headlamp, magnetic LED light, and magnetic LED wand. They're all rechargeable via a USB cable, which means that you don't have to hunt for new batteries when they die.

the engine bay, which is never a bad thing.

Many other specialty tools are available for these trucks. If the plan is to keep the stock antilock braking system (ABS) or drivetrain, consider buying a GM Tech 2 tool. These OBD-II scanning tools made by General Motors help do everything from diagnostic work to bleeding the ABS. They aren't made anymore, so find one used on eBay or pick up a clone from an off-brand vendor.

To install an aftermarket steering wheel, such as those from Billet Specialties or Budnik, the stock steering wheel must be removed. While there are ways to do it without the specialty tool (a steering-wheel puller), it is significantly easier with one. Note that a steering-wheel puller can be rented.

For the most part, other specialty tools are bought on an as-needed basis. For example, if the goal is to remove the original engine fan and replace it with an electric model, get the right tool for that job. If the original engine fan will work, don't spend the money on a new tool.

Depending on the amount of fabrication that you plan to do yourself, buying a MIG welder can be helpful. If you know how to TIG weld, have at it, but a MIG welder is great for a beginner. A MIG welder can be used one handed, and it's not as expensive as a TIG welder. In addition, it makes welding that bridge notch or shaving door handles straightforward.

Although this may be stretching the definition of being a specialty tool, lights are also pretty important. Today, flashlights and headlamps can be purchased with bright LEDs. A great option for an LED flashlight or headlamp while working on these trucks is one with a magnetic base. Cheap wand models can be found on Amazon. They charge via USB and even have adjustable outputs. Milwaukee also sells several magnetic light options—from wide ones to pen lights. While headlamps may look odd, they're effective. Most look like a workout headband with one or two LED strips that run across your forehead. These are bright and help you see exactly what you're working on. Some models even have an additional spotlight on the side too.

The front suspension on these trucks uses a coil spring, and to remove it safely, use a coil-spring compressor. Use the coil-spring compressor to compress the springs when the front suspension is taken apart. Although it takes more time, it will prevent some stress. Renting one at a local parts store can be done inexpensively, so if you're only going to do the job once, go that route.

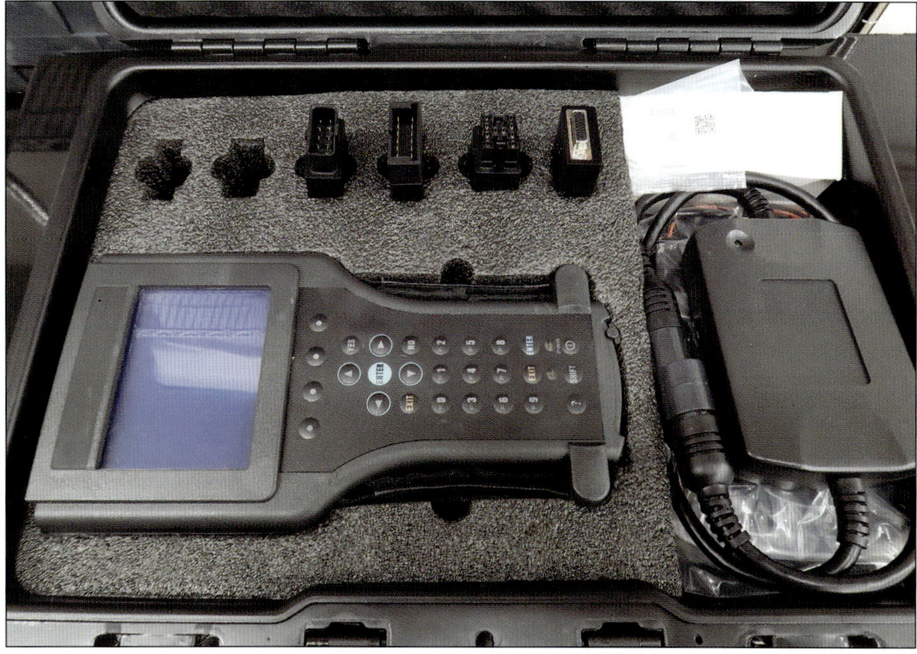

Although this isn't the genuine article, it is a GM Tech 2. It's perfect for bleeding the ABS as well as figuring out any issues with newer-model OBS trucks.

CHAPTER 4

Building the Suspension

OBS trucks are perfect for builders for many reasons, and a big one is the easy-to-work-on suspension. These trucks can be modified with bolt-on components to run coilovers or a drop. They can also run airbags with some additional tweaks. Any setup is possible—from laying it on the ground to slamming through corners. It's pretty amazing.

The first step is to determine which direction you want to go. Let's dive deeper into the suspension world to go over the options.

Steering Upgrades

The steering on these trucks can be not so great sometimes, particularly as they age. They use a recirculating-ball setup with multiple links and ball joints, and each component wears out over time. Driving one of these trucks without those parts tuned up results in a very vague sense of the road.

The problem starts at the steering shaft. This intermediate shaft goes between the steering wheel and the steering box, and it is located in the engine bay. The linkages can round out over time, and the rag joint gets tired as well. The solution is to install a new intermediate shaft, but to get really fancy, use universal joints instead of a rag joint. These are a lot tighter and don't tend to loosen over time.

The next item is the steering box itself. Your project truck may be fortunate and only have 50,000 miles on it, but most of these vehicles have over 200,000 miles, and those steering boxes feel every bit of that mileage. Replacing the box isn't difficult with the right tools. Use a Pitman-arm puller (one can be rented from an auto parts store) and be prepared to lift some heavy stuff. However, it can be done in an afternoon without too much hassle.

To upgrade the steering box, consider one from RedHead Steering Gears. They have a 2.5 quick-turn option. This means that it takes 2.5 turns of the steering wheel to go to lock (as opposed to three turns). They are available for about $300, but there's a $150 core deposit.

Then, there are the tie-rod ends. To just tighten things up, begin with the Baer Tracker tie-rod ends. These are aluminum tie-rod adjusters with Heim joints instead of ball joints. They also come with a machined bolt that's tapered perfectly for the factory spindle, which means avoiding any drilling or modifications. This reduces any slop incurred through

Look closely at the tie-rod end (below the sway bar). It's beat up. Many of these trucks have similar issues due to years of neglect. Make sure that yours isn't one of them. (Photo Courtesy Switch Suspension)

This 1998 Chevrolet Tahoe has a 4/6 drop with springs, spindles, shackles, and a flip kit. It sits on 15-inch 454 SS wheels with smaller tires in the front than in the back.

the ball joints, and it is completely a bolt-in procedure.

Of course, all of that can be thrown out, and a rack-and-pinion setup can be used. Elevated Concepts Inc. sells a kit for about $2,000 that includes a new rack, lines, hardware, bracketry, etc. for 2WD models. Although it's a bit pricey, this may be the best way to dial in the steering on your truck. Alternately, you have the option of doing the leg work and fabricating it yourself.

Sway Bar Upgrades

Almost all OBS trucks came with front sway bars installed. Keep those in place. While some people suggest to ditch the sway bar and just go with better shocks, the improved handling that is provided by connecting the front two wheels makes a dramatic difference. That, and there is a heavy engine up front. Even if you're bagging the truck, removing the sway bar is a bad idea.

However, upgrading the sway bar is wise. Using a beefier sway bar that keeps your truck flat around the curves dramatically helps the overall handling. There are many different options, and many of them mount in the factory location, which makes swapping them out straightforward. A torsion bar-style sway bar is an option in some instances, but that usually requires some fabrication.

Then, there's the rear of the truck. Most of them didn't come with a rear sway bar, so adding one will help significantly. A rear sway bar helps tie the rear suspension together. Even though you're running a straight axle, it's a nice add-on.

Lowering Kits

The 1988–1998 Chevy or GMC truck in your garage is begging for an upgrade. The most popular of which is lowering the truck to a reasonable level. How reasonable is up to you, but everything from a 2/4 to a 6/8 is possible with the correct setup.

Let's take a moment to explain those numbers. When dealing with a lowering kit for an OBS, the numbers laid out are 1/2, 2/4, 4/6, etc. The first digit is the amount of drop (in inches) for the front end of the truck. The second digit is the amount of drop for the rear of the truck.

So, why are the two numbers so different? Look at a stock truck in a parking lot sometime. You'll notice that the rear end is actually higher than the front so that the truck remains level if the bed is loaded. General Motors (and many vehicle manufacturers) actually cut the fender so that when the truck is unloaded, the gap between the tires and the fenders matches on all four corners.

So, when buying a lowering kit, unless you want a raked-out ride (a totally valid option), the rear end will sit lower than the front. If you want them the same height, just select the right kit for your needs.

There are many reasons to lower a truck. The first reason is improved handling. A lower center of gravity

The dark gray part in the middle of the image is the spindle. In this case, it's a dropped spindle from McGaughys. This provides a good 2 inches of drop while still keeping the suspension geometry intact. (Photo Courtesy Switch Suspension)

results in being able to toss the truck into corners without the fear of tipping over. The second reason is that it rides better. You can buy springs and shocks that are designed to provide a smoother ride or one that's tighter. Finally, it just looks cool. Seeing one of these trucks going down the road is pretty amazing and may even be why you bought this book.

So, where should you start? Well, there are a few different parts options to discuss, and each one has its pros and cons.

Many people begin their build with dropped spindles. These replace the stock spindles (also called steering knuckles, although that's not entirely accurate for this bodystyle) with a spindle that is relocated up higher. In this way, the geometry of the suspension remains the same, but you get the drop that you want.

Some spindles kick the wheel out 1/4 inch to 1/2 inch more than the stockers, which can limit the width of the wheels and tires that can be installed. Pro Performance sells React drop spindles, which are designed to keep everything factory (no extra track width). They're also designed for big brake kits, and a minimum of 17-inch wheels must be installed. Even those may require some trimming, depending on the wheels.

Coil springs are one of the cheapest ways to lower the front of the truck. They swap out in place of the stock version and are available in a variety of different drops. The downside is they will slightly change the suspension geometry, and that may put more wear on the ball joints, depending on the amount of drop. However, they're cheap and are usually used in combination with spindles.

Dropped control arms aren't as popular as they used to be, but they have a purpose. Most of them have a lowered spring pocket to provide the drop. Others have improved angles on the ball joints, which also helps. Today's custom control arms are often designed for airbags, coilovers, and extreme drops.

In the back, most people begin with a dropped shackle. These mount to the rear of the leaf spring and replace the stock unit. Depending on what mounting spot is used on the shackle, you can get 1 to 2 inches of drop with these. There isn't a big drawback to the process, either. The only thing to check for is a shackle that causes the leaf to hit the bottom of the bed. If that happens, the crossmember can usually be trimmed to accommodate the drop.

Dropped hanger kits are available. These do the same thing as the shackles but on the forward end of the leaf. The difficulty level is increased a bit, as the stock hangers need to be removed to install the new ones. To do that, grind an "X" shape into the heads of the rivets that hold the stock hanger in place. Then, use an air hammer with a chisel attachment to knock off the heads.

Flip kits are quite popular. They can provide 6 inches of drop, which is great for the 4/6 drop that most people choose. The difficulty level is increased, as the entire leaf spring needs to be removed from the chassis (it's quite heavy), placed under the axle, and reinstalled. That extra weight can be taxing, so keep that in mind.

Some of these kits require notching or bridging the frame to allow the axle to travel deeper into the chassis. (More information regarding notching and bridging the frame is provided later in this chapter.)

StreetGrip Install

Arguably the most popular drop that is available for these trucks is a 4/6 drop. When completed, there's no question that the truck has been lowered, and it's still completely streetable. The truck gets better handling, it looks great, and it's relatively easy to do. Plus, it is possible to pick up a kit for less than $2,000.

In the following scenario, the owner of the truck wanted a kit that performed well and looked good. A RideTech StreetGrip kit was used to give it a 4/6 drop. When combined with bigger wheels and lower-profile tires, the handling was upgraded substantially.

This is a flip kit installed on the rear end of a Chevy truck. Note the new U-bolts as well as the way that the leaf-spring mount keys into the stock one. (Photo Courtesy Switch Suspension)

Here's the truck as it began: a stock early-model GMC with the original suspension. (Photo Courtesy Switch Suspension)

This is the RideTech StreetGrip kit. It includes McGaughys spindles, new springs, a flip kit, a bolt-in C-notch, the appropriate drop shocks, and relocation brackets. (Photo Courtesy Switch Suspension)

Disassembling the Front Suspension

1 After the truck is up on the rack, remove the tie-rod ends. Remove the cotter pin and castle nut and then knock the tie-rod end out of the way with a hammer. (Photo Courtesy Switch Suspension)

2 To remove the stock shocks, unbolt them on the top of the frame. Then, unbolt the bottom two bolts on the lower control arm. Pull the shocks straight down and out. (Photo Courtesy Switch Suspension)

3 Now, separate the rotor from the spindle. To do so, unbolt the caliper and set it to the side, hanging from a metal wire. Then, remove the dust cap and unbolt the rotor from the spindle. (Photo Courtesy Switch Suspension)

Disassembling the Front Suspension *continued*

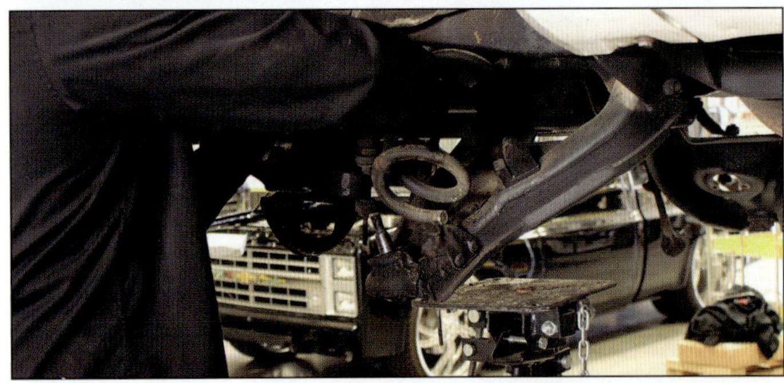

4 *With a jack underneath the lower control arm, separate the spindle from the control arms. Then, carefully lower the jack to release tension on the spring. After it's loose, pull out the spring. (Photo Courtesy Switch Suspension)*

Installing the Front Suspension

1 *Seat the new coil spring into the frame and the lower control-arm pocket by hand. Use the jack to put tension on the arm and compress the spring temporarily until the spindle is mounted. (Photo Courtesy Switch Suspension)*

2 *Next, install the McGaughys spindle. This one has been modified. (See chapter 5 for more details.) (Photo Courtesy Switch Suspension)*

3 *Install the new adjustable Fox shocks. They're tuned for handling, but the owner can change that later if desired. (Photo Courtesy Switch Suspension)*

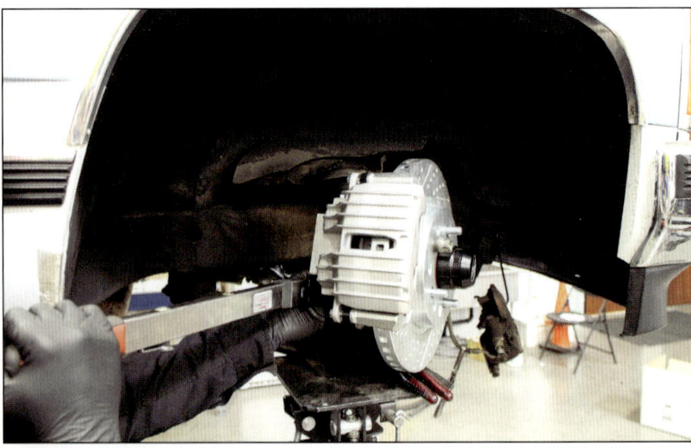

4 *With the new brakes installed, torque the bolts to their proper specifications to complete the front suspension. (Photo Courtesy Switch Suspension)*

Installing the C-Notch

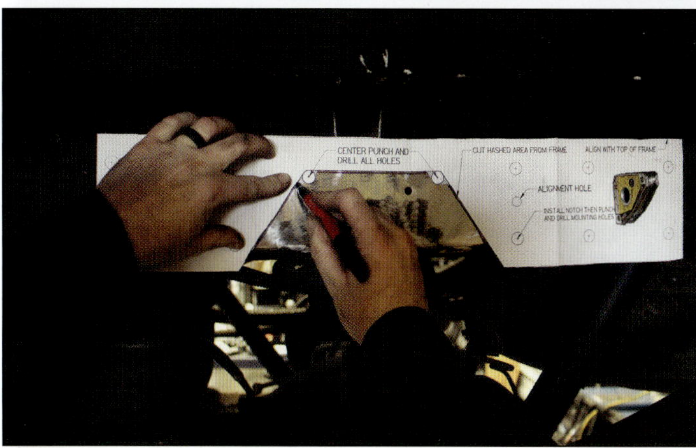

1 *One of the first steps for the back of the truck is cutting the C-notch. RideTech includes a paper template with the kit. Magnets are used to hold the template in place, and then it can be traced. (Photo Courtesy Switch Suspension)*

2 *Before cutting the notch, remove the bed cross-members above it. They'll be in the way later. (Photo Courtesy Switch Suspension)*

3 *With everything marked, notch the frame by using a cut-off wheel on a grinder. Drill holes in the corners first so that the edges there are rounded. This reduces the chance of the frame cracking on the corners. (Photo Courtesy Switch Suspension)*

4 *Use the notch as a template for the remaining bolt locations. (Photo Courtesy Switch Suspension)*

5 *Bolt the notch in place to complete this step in the process. (Photo Courtesy Switch Suspension)*

Disassembling and Installing the Rear Suspension

1 Remove the stock shocks by unbolting them from the axle and frame. (Photo Courtesy Switch Suspension)

2 Lower the leaf springs carefully to hang so that the axle can be flipped. (Photo Courtesy Switch Suspension)

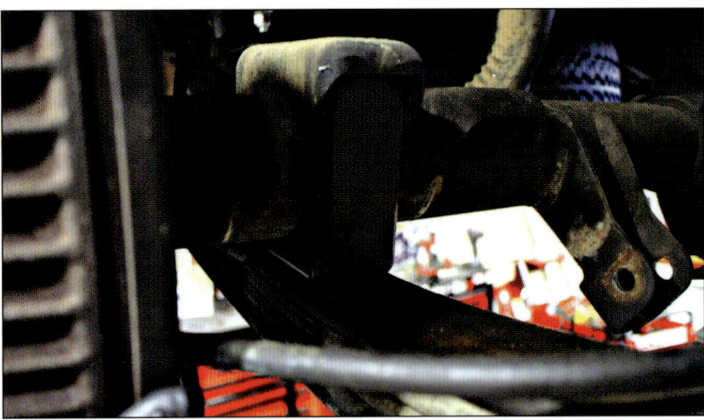

3 Next, install the flip kit. It nestles inside of the stock leaf-spring mount. (Photo Courtesy Switch Suspension)

4 To complete the axle flip, position the U-bolts and tighten the nuts against the new leaf-spring plate. (Photo Courtesy Switch Suspension)

5 The new rear shocks need to be properly aligned because the axle has been repositioned. Install shock extenders to align the rear shocks. (Photo Courtesy Switch Suspension)

6 The finishing touch is a set of 20-inch Ridler Wheels (model 605) with 295/35-20 Nitto tires. (Photo Courtesy Switch Suspension)

7 *The truck's appearance has been significantly improved. In addition, it handles well. (Photo Courtesy Switch Suspension)*

Coilovers

On one hand, there are airbags. They're the ultimate way to get a truck up and down whenever the owner would like. Then, there are static drops, which are as straightforward as one would expect: bolt on some parts to make the truck sit lower. However, if you want a hybrid that's also infinitely tunable, use coilovers. They have become very popular for good reason.

The basic idea is straightforward: replace the static suspension with a strut (a shock absorber with a coil around it). However, this strut has a threaded body so that the lower coil perch can move up and down with the aid of a pair of special wrenches. This allows the owner to fine-tune the suspension within a specified height range. Note that this fine-tuning can only be done when the vehicle is parked. So, it offers the adjustability of airbags (albeit slower) and is particularly well suited to the track.

Several companies offer full coilover conversion kits for OBS trucks. The installation process involves some cutting and removing pretty much everything. However, the results are stellar.

Coilover Install

The project truck is a 1993 Indianapolis 500 Pace truck, and it's in great shape. These trucks were mostly stock with a few tweaks, and the suspension wasn't anything exciting. In this case, the installation of a QA1 coilover kit is a substantial upgrade.

The aspect that makes a 1993 Indianapolis 500 Pace truck so special is the graphics package, and the coilover kit that will be installed will make its performance match its appearance. (Photo Courtesy Switch Suspension)

Laying Out the Kit

1 *The kit is packed with everything that is needed to install coilovers. Note all of the brackets. Those will help to replace the leaf springs in the back. (Photo Courtesy Switch Suspension)*

2 *The entire shock body of each coilover is threaded. The lower perch mount threads onto it, which provides adjustability. (Photo Courtesy Switch Suspension)*

Installing the Front Suspension

1 *With the truck on a lift, remove the front suspension. In this case, the team is upgrading the front brakes completely, so the entire spindle and brake assembly has been removed and set aside. (Photo Courtesy Switch Suspension)*

2 *Remove the coils, shocks, and control arms, leaving the frame bare and ready for new parts. (Photo Courtesy Switch Suspension)*

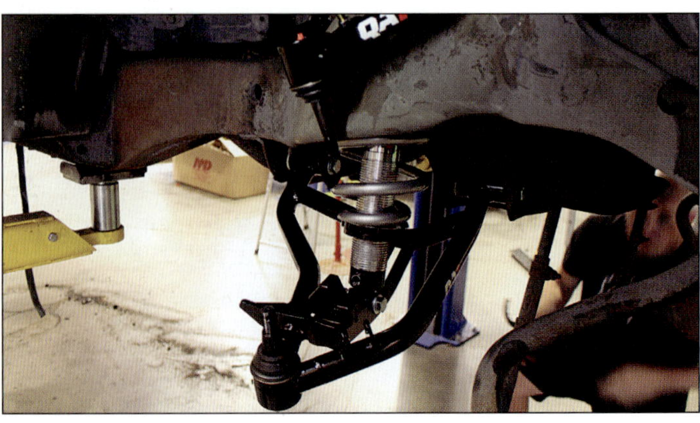

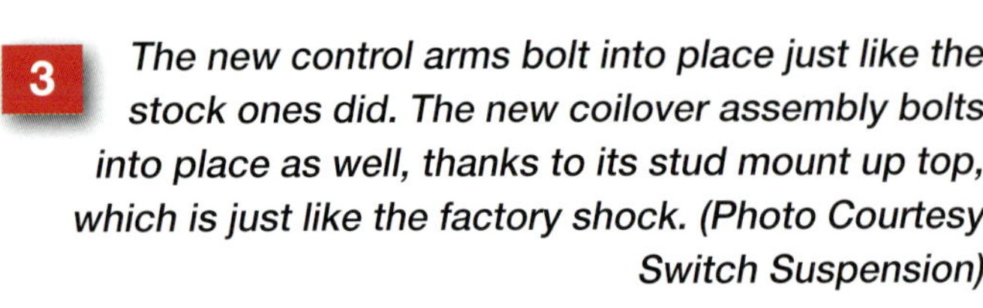

3 *The new control arms bolt into place just like the stock ones did. The new coilover assembly bolts into place as well, thanks to its stud mount up top, which is just like the factory shock. (Photo Courtesy Switch Suspension)*

Installing the Front Suspension *continued*

4 *Install the React modular dropped spindles. These are significant because most aftermarket dropped spindles widen the track width up to a 1/2 inch, which can cause problems with rubbing the tires against the fenders while turning. (Photo Courtesy Switch Suspension)*

5 *These brakes are the 14-inch Revelators from Pro Performance. They have a hub system that replaces the individual bearings and bolts to the React spindles. (Photo Courtesy Switch Suspension)*

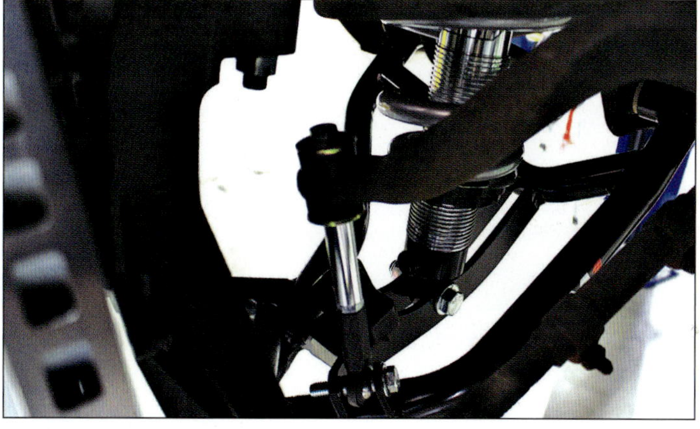

6 *Install the sway-bar end links, which mount to the lower control arm using the provided hardware. (Photo Courtesy Switch Suspension)*

Installing the Rear Suspension

1 *Instructions for the rear kit begin with marking for a C-notch. This provides the axle more room to travel in the frame so that it doesn't bottom out. The kit includes this template, which the team at Switch Suspension traces onto the frame using chalk. (Photo Courtesy Switch Suspension)*

2 *The notch is being cut out with a plasma cutter. This is the fastest and easiest way to cut through the thick steel frame, but it could also be done with a grinder or a reciprocating saw. (Photo Courtesy Switch Suspension)*

Installing the Rear Suspension *continued*

3 *Mount the notch plate, which also includes the upper coilover mounts. After it's centered on the notch and the marked holes, mark the remaining holes onto the frame and drill them out. (Photo Courtesy Switch Suspension)*

4 *Here's the completed notch bolted in place. (Photo Courtesy Switch Suspension)*

5 *At this point, some factory parts must be removed. This includes the leaf-spring hangers, and they're riveted in place. There are two options for taking them off. One option is to cut an "X" into the head with a grinder and then use an air hammer with a chisel attachment to knock out the rivets. (Photo Courtesy Switch Suspension)*

6 *The second option is to use a plasma cutter or torch to burn out the rivets. Then, they can be knocked out with an air hammer. Either way, the upper shock mounts and spring perches must be removed. (Photo Courtesy Switch Suspension)*

7 *The driver-side C-notch comes with this bracket built in. This coilover kit has many links to keep the rear end solidly in place, and this particular mount is great for lateral support. (Photo Courtesy Switch Suspension)*

8 *Replace the forward leaf-spring mounts with these mounts for the linkage. They're adjustable so that the truck can be properly aligned. (Photo Courtesy Switch Suspension)*

9 The links mount to brackets that sit on the axle where the leaf springs bolted up. (Photo Courtesy Switch Suspension)

10 They also hold the lower coilover mounts, which keeps the coils vertical. (Photo Courtesy Switch Suspension)

11 The rear end receives a new, crab-like mount that replaces the differential cover. Multiple links connect here as well to keep the axle positioned properly. (Photo Courtesy Switch Suspension)

12 Mount the lateral linkage in place. These links are adjustable for alignment purposes. (Photo Courtesy Switch Suspension)

13 Some brackets are included that mount to the frame. They not only stiffen the chassis but also provide a mounting location for the axle linkage. (Photo Courtesy Switch Suspension)

14 With all of the various linkages mounted to the brackets, this is the result. It's complex, yes. However, it gives the truck a solid grip on the road. (Photo Courtesy Switch Suspension)

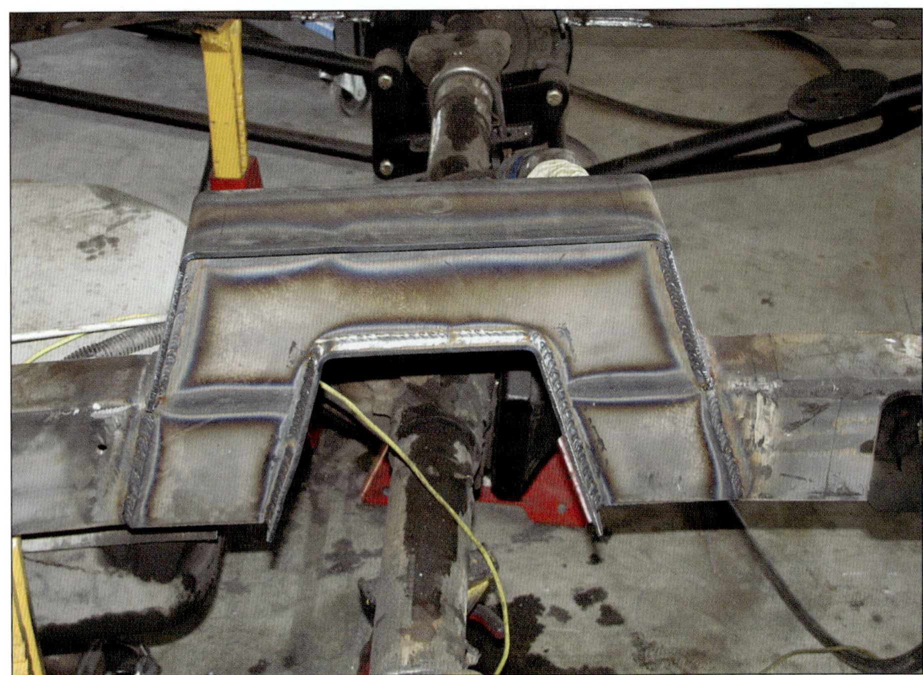

Check out this bridge notch. This is an 8-piece kit, and it provides a lot of flexibility for installation. It is welded in place and is very strong.

This is a bolt-in C-notch. It provides extra travel for the suspension but is simple to install with a few basic tools. (Photo Courtesy Ruben Castañon)

C-Notches and Bridge Notches

If you peek underneath the rear of a stock 1988–1998 truck, you'll see a straight axle that is supported by leaf springs and dampened by shocks. Those leaf springs traditionally sit on top of the axle. Look at the distance between the axle tubing and the frame. This is now your point of focus.

If you're lowering the truck, the distance between the axle tubing and the frame will be shorter. Eventually, the axle tube will be too close to the frame. If you ever put something in the bed to carry home from the hardware store or hit too big of a bump, the axle tube would hit the steel (or the bumpstop that was designed to slow down that action). In addition, it would result in a very rough ride. More clearance is needed, and that is the reason for a C-notch or bridge notch.

In its most simple state, a C-notch is a C-shaped hole that is cut into the stock chassis and then reinforced with steel to ensure that the frame doesn't sag or split. It's shaped like a "C" because the axle is a round tube, and that allows the axle to go higher into the frame.

Many C-notch kits are designed to be very user friendly. They're bolt-in affairs with cardboard templates and instructions that don't require much more than a drill and a cutting tool. The well-designed ones are so precise that you don't have to stress about locating it correctly. However, make sure to do the job correctly. Otherwise, issues can present themselves in the future.

The biggest potential problems with a C-notch are weakness in the frame and cracks. When cutting a notch, sometimes it leaves two straight lines joining together. This connection can eventually form a crack. Instead, if you drill a hole and then connect the straight lines into that hole, this decreases the probability of cracking. Regarding weakness, a good C-notch kit has thick enough steel to handle that problem on its own. Even better kits sandwich two pieces of steel together, providing a beefier connection than the truck had from the factory.

If you want to go even lower than what a C-notch will provide, look into a bridge notch (also called a bridge). These are larger structures that are designed to span a gap that is cut into the frame. The idea is that they will still provide the strength that is needed and allow substantially more travel in the process.

How do you build one? It begins with 2x4-inch steel tubing that is at least 1/8-inch thick. The tubing goes up from the frame at about a 45-degree angle, straightens out, and then returns to the frame. The idea is that when you're done, you'll just cut out the part in the middle.

Alternatively, some kits are made of plates. First, you weld the plates to the frame. Then, you connect them all. The result is a completed notch that won't jeopardize the integrity of the stock chassis while you install it.

If the plan is to only have a lowered stance, chances are good that a bridge isn't needed. However, if you're considering a four-link suspension with coilovers or even bagging your ride, a bridge notch is in your future.

These kinds of setups provide more than just additional axle clearance. Since the bridge notch is taller (and it can be set as tall as needed), it can be used to make mounts for other things. Crossbars that connect the two notches that hold the shocks are popular, and they are required for the best kind of coilover setup. You can also weld the shock mounts to the outside of the notch so that it's more outboard on the chassis. This cuts down on the width of wheel that can be run, but the truck will handle better.

Although it's not a key point, it's also important to note that you can get creative with crossmembers and bridge-notch design as a whole. While the structural integrity needs to remain intact, there's no reason to not add some flair. The upper bag mounts on bag-over-axle setups often have tribal designs worked into their plates, which gives the truck a unique appearance. In addition, it is possible to work in a fifth-wheel hitch for a dually or something similar.

One other item to note is that many notches (a C-notch or a bridge) require bed modification. After all, if the axle is traveling farther up into the chassis, something will eventually hit the floor of the bed.

Usually, this is the pumpkin. The center portion of the axle has the highest profile, and you can get away with notching the bed floor crossmember to provide enough clearance. However, if you are doing a bridge notch of almost any size, the bed floor must be cut out to accommodate the axle and the frame. This may also apply to the fender wells, depending on the size of the wheels and tires.

Many people opt to keep the bed floor open to show off their intricate designs or the details on the frame. However, to use the bed, it will need a cover. The best option is to create a sheet-metal panel that's removable. By using a panel, the suspension can still be accessed by removing a few screws, but the truck can still be used like a truck without worrying about stuff falling through a hole in the floor.

There is another option, but it's a lot more labor intensive. That option is to body drop the bed. This is discussed in depth later in the book, but the basic idea is to cut out the floor of the truck bed and relocate it up higher in the overall box. This provides more clearance for the frame and under-bed accessories, but it also keeps the entire floor straight. Yes, the bed will have a diminished capacity. After all, it means taking out at least 4 inches from the overall depth, so there is some kind of loss. However, if you get a factory-looking bed out of the deal, is that worth complaining about?

Body dropping the bed isn't a quick process, and it involves a lot of welding. Although, if you want a bed floor that's free of holes, consider this path.

Chassis Swap Options

If you really want to go big, consider an entirely new chassis. This has an entirely new frame, so it's no small undertaking. The suspension, brake lines, and electrical will all be replaced. The result is a setup that's exactly how you want it, and that's pretty cool.

It is possible to fabricate a chassis or buy one from vendors, including Choppin' Block and GSI. They vary greatly in price, and they are usually a build-on-demand item, which means that there may be a wait to get what you want.

Either way, a full chassis is a neat way to start fresh and get your truck exactly where you want it to sit.

The Low-Pro Chassis

While there are many custom chassis kits out there, the hot ticket recently has been the OBS Low-Pro chassis from Roadster Shop. It starts at $40,000, so it's not cheap, but the result is impressive.

For years, there have been two types of chassis out there: a coilover model and one that allows airbags. However, this Low-Pro chassis also sits the truck down dramatically lower over the frame, has an independent rear suspension, and doesn't require cutting out the bed floor. It can be customized to within an inch of its life—from the brakes to the powder coating and more. Basically, this is the setup for putting an OBS on the ground and getting it to handle like a dream. ■

This is Jeff Volker's 1993 Chevrolet Silverado Indy 500 Pace Truck's new chassis: the Low-Pro from the Roadster Shop. (Photo Courtesy Jeff Volker)

This chassis has an independent rear end and is designed so that the bed isn't cut and yet you can still run a 31-inch-tall tire in the back. (Photo Courtesy Jeff Volker)

In the front, the upper shock mounts flow into the frame and can still fit a 29-inch front wheel and tire combination. (Photo Courtesy Jeff Volker)

CHAPTER 5

Brakes

OBS trucks came from the factory with front disc brakes and rear drum brakes. Earlier trucks don't have ABS, but the newer models do. These are big, heavy trucks with big, heavy motors, and increasing the stopping power is always good.

Fortunately, many options are available for improvement. If you only want to tweak the brakes without doing anything drastic, upgrade the rotors and brake pads. Little Shop Mfg. offers a kit for the front end that includes cross-drilled rotors and new pads for less than $300. You can add new calipers as well. You just need to know whether you have the 1- or 1.25-inch-wide calipers, and that is easy to determine.

Brake line upgrades are another option. The stock units that go from the hard line to the caliper are made of rubber, and they deteriorate over time. They also flex, causing a loss in pressure. Stainless-steel brake lines don't flex, so when the pedal is put down, all of that force is applied directly to the calipers.

EBC Brakes makes improved brake pads. They have everything from track-tested models to those that are better suited for the everyday cruiser that just needs to slow down faster.

Of course, to really beef up the brakes, you need to go with something bigger.

Front Disc Brake Upgrades

The best way to upgrade the front disc brakes is to use a big brake kit. These are available from various vendors, including Little Shop Mfg., Pro Performance, etc.

There are a few things to consider before installing a big break kit. Let's start with the wheels. Most big brake kits won't fit over the stock 15-inch wheels, so it is necessary to upgrade to something larger. For most, that won't be a problem because larger wheels were likely always part of the plan. However, it is something to consider. For example, Little Shop Mfg. offers a 14-inch brake upgrade for these trucks, and it will only work on an 18-inch (or larger) wheel. Little Shop Mfg. also offers a 16-inch version, and that only fits most 20-inch (or larger) wheels.

Another factor to consider is cost. A front disc big-brake upgrade can cost upward of $2,500. If the plan is to build a custom truck with rims that show off the brakes, it's definitely an upgrade to consider.

Big Brake Kit Installation

A GMC truck that received a StreetGrip setup from RideTech was featured in chapter 4. At that same time, it had a new set of brakes (front and rear) installed to complement the suspension. It is a great combination.

This front brake kit that was used is sold by Pro Performance, and it's called the 14-inch Revelator system. It includes everything needed to get the job done in just a few hours.

The spindle must be modified to fit the new calipers. If that makes you nervous, use a React spindle, as that negates that requirement.

Prepping for the Front Brakes

1 This is the 14- and 13-inch Revelator suspension kit for OBS trucks. It's a full front and rear kit, and it will be installed on the GMC that was featured in last chapter's StreetGrip install. (Photo Courtesy Switch Suspension)

2 The new caliper bracket needs to mount to the spindle, but the existing mounting points are in the way. (Photo Courtesy Switch Suspension)

3 With the spindle in a vise, cut off the marked areas with a grinder. (Photo Courtesy Switch Suspension)

4 Re-tap two of the holes to accommodate the new mounting hardware. (Photo Courtesy Switch Suspension)

5 After the spindle is reinstalled onto the front suspension, torque the bracket into place. (Photo Courtesy Switch Suspension)

Installing the Front Brakes

1 *Install the Revelator hub. This replaces the original bearing system and makes for a cleaner install. (Photo Courtesy Switch Suspension)*

2 *After the rotor has been slipped over the hub, install the new dust cap. Keep everything aligned by tightening down a lug nut. You can see how the caliper bracket sits compared to the spindle and the rotor. (Photo Courtesy Switch Suspension)*

3 *Install the caliper and torque it down to complete the front-end install. (Photo Courtesy Switch Suspension)*

Rear Disc Brake Conversion

Although upgrading the front brakes is a worthy improvement, a bigger flex is to do a rear disc brake conversion. This improves braking substantially, and it looks significantly better as well.

If you're thinking about making the switch to discs, consider other modifications that you want to do to the rear end at the same time. The axle shafts often must be removed as part of the rear disc brake conversion, so if you want to change the gears, fix the bearings, or do anything else, your chance is now.

Prepping for the Rear Brakes

1 *The first step is to drain the differential and remove the cover. (Photo Courtesy Switch Suspension)*

2 *There's a locking pin in the gearset that needs to be removed. Unbolt it and slide it out of the housing. (Photo Courtesy Switch Suspension)*

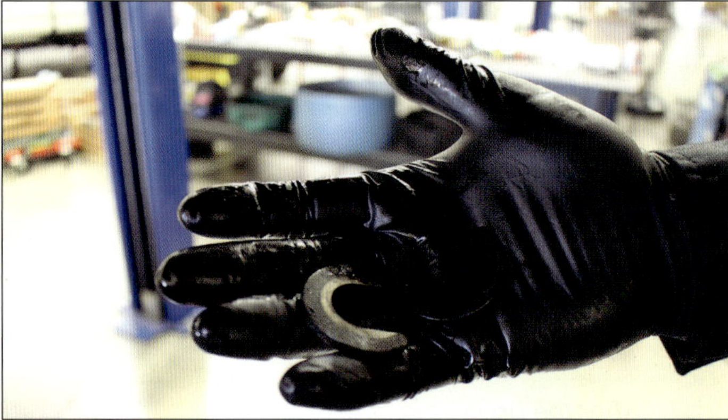

3 *There's one C-clip per axle shaft in the rear end. To free them, just push on the end and they should fall out. A tool with a magnetic tip helps here too. (Photo Courtesy Switch Suspension)*

4 *After the C-clips have been removed, slide the axle shafts out of the housing. (Photo Courtesy Switch Suspension)*

5 *Unbolt the drums by undoing the backing plate. After the brake line is free, pull off the whole unit. (Photo Courtesy Switch Suspension)*

Installing the Disc Brake Conversion Kit

1 Bolt in the brackets for the new calipers. (Photo Courtesy Switch Suspension)

2 After the bracket is in place, slide the axle shafts back in and reinstall them. Don't forget to refill the differential when done. (Photo Courtesy Switch Suspension)

3 The rotor slides right onto the axle shaft and is held in place temporarily with a few lug nuts. (Photo Courtesy Switch Suspension)

4 Install the caliper and optional emergency-brake bracket and torque them to spec. (Photo Courtesy Switch Suspension)

5 Run stainless-steel brake lines from the caliper to the factory rear brake line. These won't flex like the factory rubber ones did. (Photo Courtesy Switch Suspension)

The ABS Problem

Many of these trucks came standard with ABS, and, unfortunately, it's not great. A huge complaint with the OBS trucks is a squishy pedal, and it seems like no matter what you do, it's difficult to get all of the air out of the system. This is particularly problematic when upgrading the lines and increasing the size of the rotors because everything is now open to the air, and it's even more difficult to remove.

There are a few different solutions. The path you take depends on your level of expertise and how much courage you have.

The first option is to completely remove the ABS system. Now this may be on the list anyway, if you're planning to body drop the truck or cut out the fender wells. While it is possible to relocate the ABS module, it's not always easy to do, and it doesn't lend itself to a clean installation unless you're redoing a bunch of brake lines. Hiding it results in similar problems.

Removing it can work if you're handy with a tubing bender and line-flaring tool. Begin by making new lines going from the master cylinder and running into the stock lines that roll out to each end of the truck. Soft lines can be used, but it's generally a best practice to use hard lines in this situation.

The second option is to see if the ABS system can be rebuilt. The problem is that when they get older, the seals tend to rot and leak. Although these trucks are popular, there isn't necessarily a huge contingent of companies that rebuild ABS systems. The computers are prone to problems, and some people complain that the issue isn't with the seals in the module but instead with corrosion in the electrical connections. Either way, those things should be fixed and/or rebuilt.

Third, and arguably the option to try first, is to bleed the ABS system. As it turns out, General Motors had a special tool for the job (and many other tasks) called the GM Tech2 tool. Getting your hands on one is another matter.

There are a few companies that make knockoffs of the tool, and many of them are based overseas. If you don't have any concerns about that, you can purchase one for around $300. However, if you only want original GM parts, then you'll need to get one on eBay, and they run anywhere from $300 to $1,700. You'll want the right connection to your OBD-II port and the proper software too. Basically, this whole scenario is kind of a mess, but if you can properly bleed your brakes as a result, look at it as a win.

Bleeding ABS Brake Systems

If you've decided to go down this path. Get that GM Tech2 tool ready to go.

Prepping for the ABS Bleeding Procedure

Before beginning the process, make sure that the brake-fluid level is good and that the parking brake is set. Shift the transmission into park or neutral.

Using the Tech 2 Tool

Make sure that the truck is running so that the Tech 2 tool can get power.

To begin the process, the truck needs to be lifted so that all four wheels are off the ground.

In this case, a QuickJack 7000TLX is being used. It costs about $2,000.

The OBD-II port is located on the driver's side of the truck underneath the knee panel. It's pretty prominent. Plug one side of the GM Tech 2 tool cable into this port.

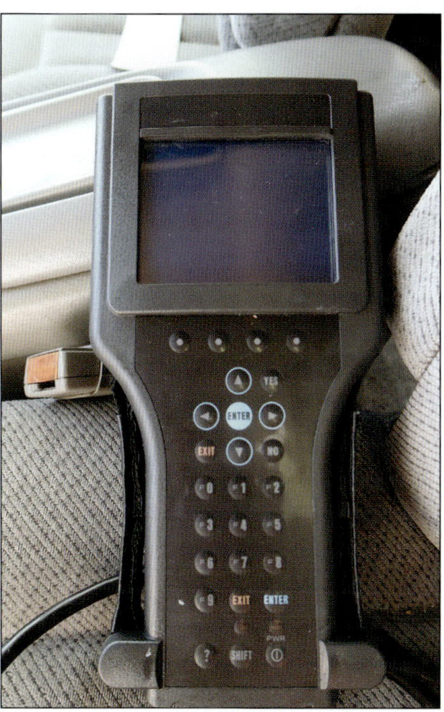

The other side should plug into the Tech 2 tool, which looks roughly like this.

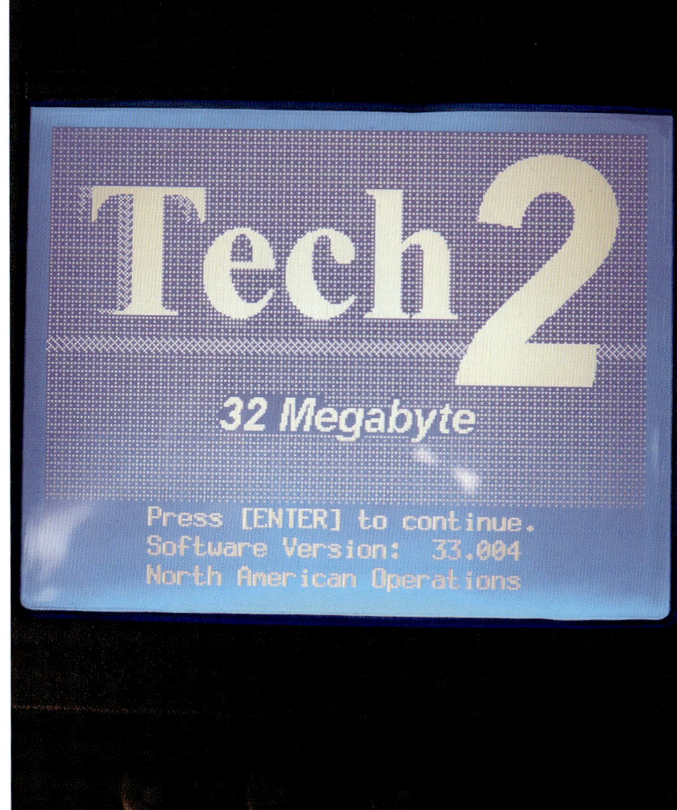

Once plugged into power, this screen will be displayed. Hit the enter button to continue.

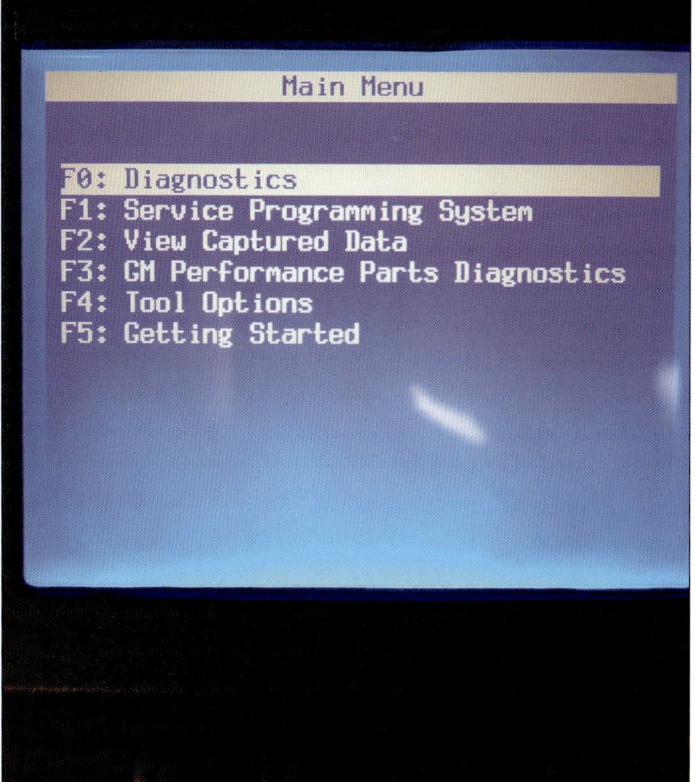

In the main menu, select "F0: Diagnostics." To proceed anywhere in this system, just hit the enter button unless otherwise noted.

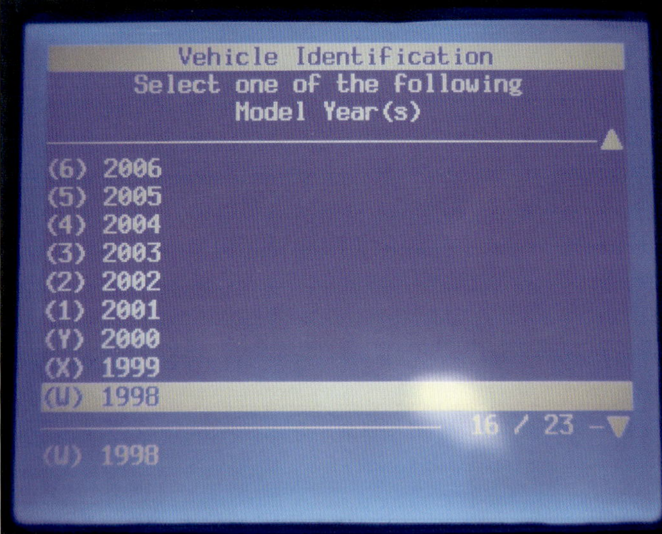

Select the year of the truck (or SUV). In this case, it's 1998.

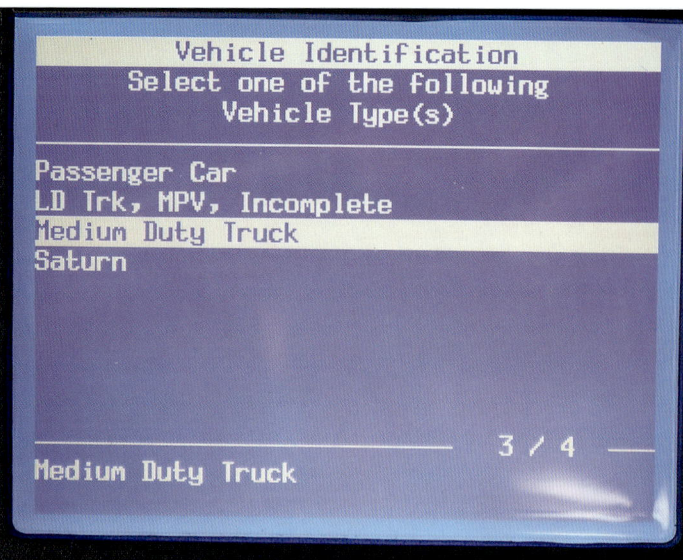

This truck is a Tahoe, so "Medium Duty Truck" is the most appropriate selection. "LD Trk" may also work, depending on your situation.

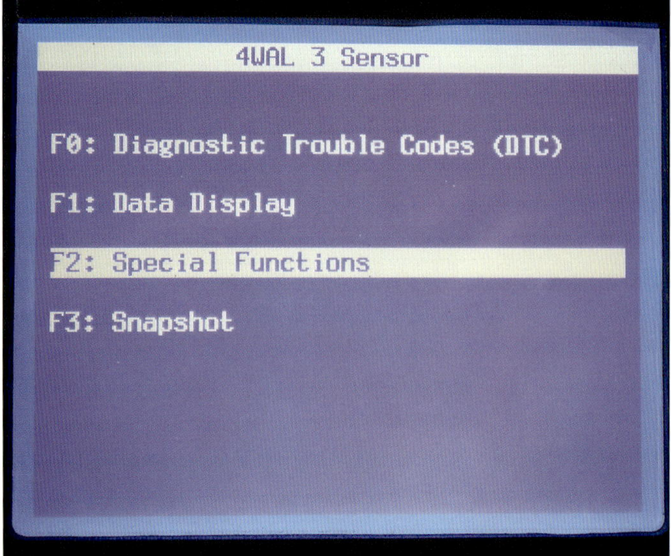

There will be one option on the next screen, so select that. Then, select the third option down called "Special Functions."

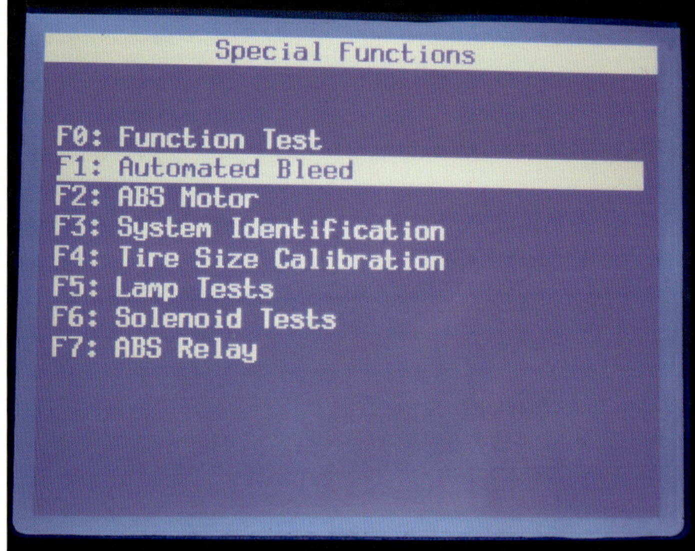

Select "F1: Automated Bleed." Click through another quick acceptance window. Then, it will say to hold down on the brake pedal. When you do, the process begins.

Air Ride Suspension

Three suspension options are available for OBS trucks: a static drop, coilovers, and fully adjustable suspension.

With a static drop, the truck is lowered to one set height. An example is a 4/6 drop. Coilovers lower the truck, but the height is adjustable. The rear leaf springs can also be replaced with a link setup, and these new shock and spring assemblies provide adjustability and the ability to fine-tune your ride. Fully adjustable suspension can be achieved with hydraulics or airbags, but in today's custom truck world, airbags are the best option. They provide flexibility and a great ride. In addition, if they are properly installed with the correct equipment, they are relatively problem free. Airbags are not inexpensive, but the results are worth the cost.

This chapter provides an overview of what airbags are and how they function, but there is enough information on this topic to fill an entire book. So, if you're looking a detailed reference that covers every facet of air ride suspensions, read *How to Install Air Ride Suspension Systems*, which I also wrote for CarTech.

Basics

Airbags operate within a system that is fairly easy to understand. An air compressor captures air from the atmosphere, compresses it, and delivers it into a storage system (an air tank in this instance). Air lines deliver the compressed air to valves that direct the air to the airbags. Then, the airbags inflate and deflate to raise and lower the vehicle. It's simple, right?

Well, it's more complicated in reality, particularly when dealing with digital air management systems. So, the simplest way to begin is to discuss the fundamental building block of an air management system: the airbags.

Airbags

In suspension terms, an airbag functions similar to a coil spring. It's an adjustable spring, and it is installed in place of a coil in a scenario where a coil is needed. It supports the weight of the vehicle just like a spring, but it does not control the oscillation of the suspension—that's the job of a shock absorber. Airbags usually have a thick, rubber bellows design, but they come in all shapes and sizes.

OBS trucks are particularly well suited for airbags. In the front, they use a control-arm setup with a coil spring, and that spring can be easily swapped with an airbag. In the rear, virtually anything can be done (from a 2-link to a parallel 4-link), and it'll function with airbags.

However, it's not all simple. You will need to fabricate some parts in the rear, cut the frame in the front,

This is a Slam Specialties SS-08 airbag. It's a double-convoluted airbag, which means that it has two bellows that make up its shape. This airbag can be used in the front, rear, or both on a truck, depending on how much space is available.

After the label is removed, the two mounting holes and the port are visible. In this case, it's a 1/2-inch NPT. Use a 1/2-inch NPT to 1/2-inch PTC or compression fitting here, or you could reduce the air line size if desired.

and possibly notch the cab. There's work to be done to fit the airbags, but it's worth it. Just know what you're getting into before you dive in.

Compressors

The airbags need air to be able to lift the truck. That air comes from a tank, but to build and compress the air, at least one compressor is required. These small devices work just like the air compressor in your garage but on a smaller scale.

There is a lot to know about compressors. Cubic feet per minute (CFM) is the amount of air that a compressor moves in 60 seconds. Pounds per square inch (PSI) is the unit of measurement used when referring to a compressor's maximum pressure production capability. It is also a number that is referenced on the airbags. These are a few of the many terms to learn before you begin.

This information is applicable for building any vehicle with an air ride suspension. With a 1988–1998 Chevrolet or GMC truck, fewer variables are involved.

Although it's possible to get away with less, use at least one compressor that's capable of producing 200 psi reliably. A good example is the Viair 485C Gen 2 compressor, which produces 200 psi and 3.82 cfm. That means it can take a 5-gallon tank from 100 percent empty to 200 psi in 4 minutes and 50 seconds or from 165 to 200 psi in 1 minute and 15 seconds. That second number is the more important one, as it's what you'll likely deal with on a regular basis.

The Viair 485C Gen 2 is available from companies such as Switch Suspension for about $410 each in platinum or stealth black. A dual compressor pack can be purchased for about $540. Viair is the gold standard in vehicle air compressors, so consider that option.

This is a Viair 310SS compressor, which is part of Viair's Stealth series. These are quiet compressors, and while they don't move air as fast as the company's other models, their low decibel rating is very much appreciated, particularly when they're underneath a bed floor.

Every compressor needs a leader hose. That's because the air coming out is hot, and a plastic line connected to the end of it would melt just from the temperature. These leader hoses are strong enough to handle the heat, and they are flexible enough to move as the compressor vibrates.

While it is possible to install more compressors, you will reach a point of diminishing returns at some point. Although it looks cool to have four compressors in the back of the bed, they pull a fair amount of current, and that can stress the charging system. It's your call, but the sweet spot on these trucks tends to be two compressors and 5 to 10 gallons of air storage. Your mileage may vary.

Pressure Switches

The pressure switch is another critical component in the compressor lineup. After a compressor has been turned on, there must be a way for it to know when to stop compressing air. Otherwise, it would just keep on doing its job until it burns up or the tank explodes.

Obviously neither of those outcomes are ideal, which is why a pressure switch is required. It's a fitting that plumbs into the air tank and has two wires coming off its end. One wire goes to 12-volt power, and the other goes to a relay that connects to a compressor (or compressors). These pressure switches have on/off ratings. For example, say that one is rated at 165 psi on and 200 psi off. When the pressure in the tank dips below 165 psi, the pressure switch will turn on, triggering the relay to activate and power the compressor. When the pressure in the tank hits 200 psi, the switch turns off, disconnecting power to the relay and shutting down the compressor.

(This is also how to determine if a pressure switch is going bad. If the compressors keep running past the "off" rating, then the switch may need replacement. The same applies if it doesn't turn on below the "on" rating.)

As a result, finding the correct pressure switch for your setup is crucial. If a pressure switch turns on and off at too low of a PSI, there won't be enough power to lift the truck—and these trucks are heavy. However, if the PSI is too high for the compressor, it could push it to an early demise.

When in doubt, ask your supplier. Employees at Switch Suspension and Lowboy Motorsports know their stuff, and they can recommend the best pairing for your situation. There's also a massive community of airbag and OBS enthusiasts on Instagram and YouTube. Look under "#OBS" to discover a wealth of knowledge.

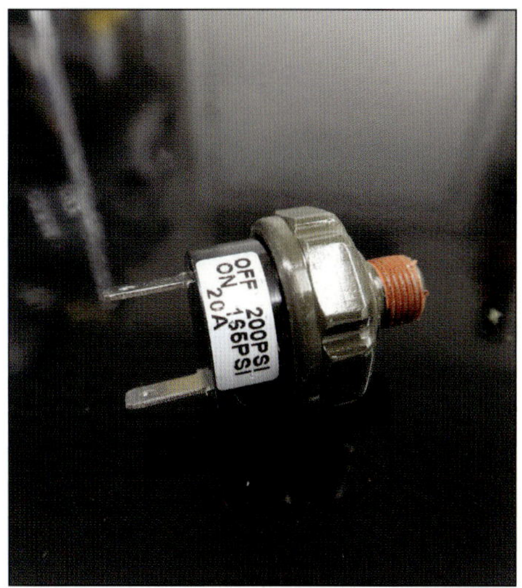

A pressure switch such as this one from Viair aways has its "Off" and "On" pressures listed. In addition, it has a threaded end to go into the tank (complete with sealant) and two electrical connections at the end for wiring purposes.

Valves, Fittings, Lines, and Tanks

After covering airbags, compressors, and pressure switches, it's now time to find a way to get the air from the tank to the airbags. To that end, a combination of products is needed.

Valves

Think of an air valve as a pen with a button on the end. When the end is clicked, the ball point pops out, and you can write. Click the pen end again to retract the ball point, and you can't write anymore. A valve operates in a similar fashion.

When an air valve that is used in an airbag setup is powered on, air flows from the source to its new destination. When the valve is inactive, it shuts and doesn't allow air to pass. Therefore, it's a normally closed valve.

Valves can be placed in several different scenarios, but typically they're used in pairs. The first valve directs air to the airbag from the tank. The second

This is an old-school valve setup, with the lift and lower valves plumbed together. The valves themselves are the fittings with the black boxes on top.

valve takes the air from the airbag and releases it into the atmosphere.

Air valves come in three forms: individually, as part of a manifold, and contained within another vessel.

An air-valve manifold is basically a chunk of aluminum with multiple valves in one body. The idea is that air is fed into the inlet, it travels through the manifold, and the valves direct it to where it needs to go. These manifolds are much more compact than individual valves, and they don't require many fittings. As a result, the probability of leaking is lower, and they can be installed in a variety of locations.

As for those that are contained within another vessel, the AccuAir ENDO-VT is a good example. With the AccuAir ENDO-VT, the valves are inside of an air tank, and all that is visible are the fittings on the end. The AirLift Performance 3P/3H setup also has the valve manifold combined with the ECU for the system.

Both of those options are expensive—at least on the surface. A Chad Criss manifold costs about $475, which has everything that is required to control the four corners of a truck. An AccuAir VU4 with 1/4-inch ports costs about $450. However, an individual valve costs only $50. The setup requires eight of them for a total of $400, which saves you at least $50. That's better, right? Well sure, until you consider the fittings that are required with individual valves.

Fittings

Almost every component in an airbag system has a fitting or a port for one. The air tank has multiple options to receive fittings. The pressure switch is threaded to go into a tank. In addition, the valves require fittings to connect to each other and to the air tank.

To paint a broad brush, fittings generally come in either National Pipe Tapered (NPT) thread or as a connection for air lines (compression or push-to-connect). An NPT fitting requires thread sealant to lock it into place, whereas an air-line fitting does not.

NPT fittings are finicky; there's no way around it. It's easy to overtighten them, which causes leaks. However, they also leak if they aren't tightened enough. While traditional red Loctite, Loctite 545, or even Teflon tape can be used, all of them can be messy and awkward to apply.

Your setup will have NPT fittings. However, if individual valves are used, the setup will require many fittings. Each one of those fittings not only adds expense but also presents an opportunity for leakage. So, to go back to the previous point about individual valves, by the time you add together the cost of all of the fittings you'll need, a manifold is a more affordable option.

Air-line fittings are much easier to work with. Push-to-connect (PTC) fittings require pushing the line into the fitting, and it's tight. That's everything, really. Also, if D.O.T.–approved fittings are used, there is even more peace of mind.

Compression fittings work like they do in the home plumbing world. They tighten down a sleeve over a line to lock it in place. However, they're one-time use (unless they're made by Swagelok), so make sure that you know what you're doing before locking them down.

Lines

Speaking of air lines, let's address them. They are available in a variety of sizes for various uses. For example, for a truck to lift up and down quickly, use 1/2- or 3/4-inch lines. This requires increasing the size of all the connections as well (valves, air tank, etc.). Otherwise, it creates a choke point, and it will slow down.

This is a PTC bulkhead fitting. Use this if you mount your tanks in the bed of the truck but want to run lines through the floor cleanly.

If speed isn't a concern, use something as straightforward as a 1/4- or 3/8-inch line. These are popular, as digital air management systems such as those from AccuAir have come into vogue.

Lines are either hard or soft. Hard lines are made from stainless steel or aluminum, and they function like the brake lines on a truck. It takes special tools to make them fit, but with some practice, you can lay them out yourself.

A major advantage of using hard lines is their durability. Once installed, there's no need to worry about puncturing them or finding one that is drooping down. In addition, some pretty cool patterns can be made with them, which makes the install look even better. The learning curve for installation is the downside, but it's something that you can figure out. *How to Install Air Ride*

Suspension Systems has an in-depth section about installing hard lines if you're interested.

Soft lines are the most common (by far). They can be purchased for less than $1 per foot or even less if you use a smaller diameter. They're easy to install, they work with PTC and compression fittings, and they are durable (if you get D.O.T.–approved lines).

The best attribute of using soft lines is their ease of installation. They can be secured to the frame with rubber or plastic clamps or even zip ties. It makes plumbing a truck a fast proposition. In addition, if you just want to test to ensure that the bags are installed properly, using soft lines to create a temporary lift system with shop air works well.

The downside comes down to how they're mounted. Soft lines flex when they air up, so they really need to be secured well. If they rub against anything, they will puncture. In addition, if cheap lines that aren't D.O.T. approved are used, the failure risk is increased. Go ahead and pony up for the better versions, as it's worth every penny.

Cover the soft lines with wire loom. This provides a few extra layers of protection, and if they do start to rub through, the problem can be solved before a leak develops.

Tanks

Air tanks store the air for the system. The options include one large tank or multiple small tanks, and it's up to you. As long as the tanks are tied together, they can be used as a collective source for the valves and bags.

The type of tank may not seem like it is important, but it is. It needs all of the right ports to connect the valves, pressure switch, and other accessories, such as water traps. They must be the correct size for your setup. To move fast, larger ports are needed on the tank too. Otherwise, they slow down the whole system.

The makeup of the tank is also important. They are available in stainless steel, aluminum, and steel. Avoid steel tanks. The air that comes out of the compressor is hot, and it will create condensation inside the tank. If steel is used, it will eventually rust out. It may take years, and it depends a lot on the type of environment that the truck is in regularly, but it's just a matter of time. Aluminum and most stainless-steel tanks don't have this issue.

There is an option that not only reduces the number of parts that are needed and provides a cleaner overall appearance: the AccuAir ENDO-VT. AccuAir released its ENDO line a few years ago in two configurations. The ENDO-T is a tank like any other, but it has a clean mounting system that results in a nice and stealthy installation. The ENDO-VT adds valves to the equation. The valves and tank come in one unit, which is not only convenient but also looks better.

The ENDO-VT starts at about $870 for the 3-gallon model. However, if you think about how much the valves cost and then factor in the added space savings, the ENDO-VT starts to look pretty good.

As of this writing, AccuAir offers the ENDO-VT in a four-valve setup, but there was previously a two-valve option as well. The two-valve setup is nice for running two smaller tanks mounted to the sides of the frame rails. Ultimately, a four-valve setup that is potentially paired with an ENDO-T is the best option on OBS trucks.

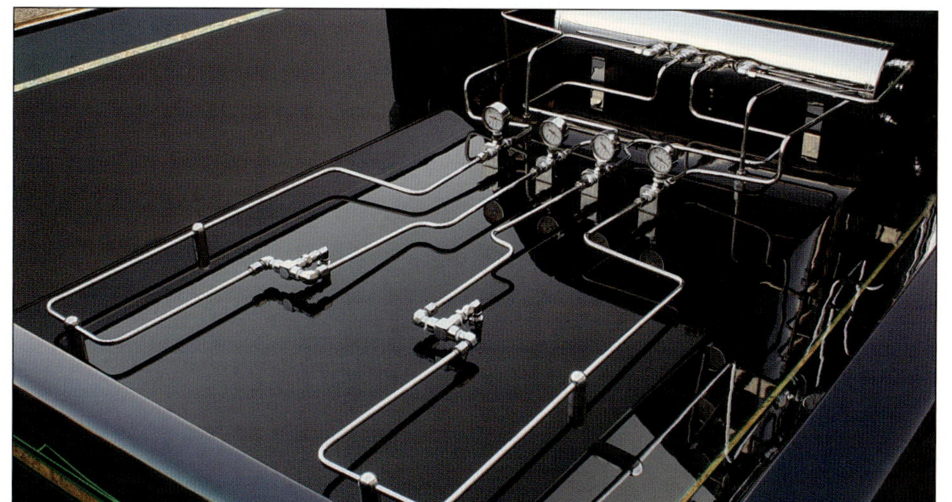

The hard lines in the bed of this truck have been chromed.

Digital Air Management Systems

Although airbags have been available for decades, one problem has been persistent: trucks and cars wouldn't lift up to a consistent height every time. People would install gauges all over their ride to try to figure out where their truck should sit, but there were too many variables. If there was a passenger, the right side wouldn't lift the same way. If the weather changed, more PSI may be needed to lift the same amount. Even eating too much at lunch could affect things. It just wasn't consistent.

Then came the rise of digital air

management systems, such as those made by AccuAir and Air Lift Performance. A few versions are available, but the basic idea is the same: provide a way to lift the vehicle to a preset height and keep it there.

The first versions were PSI based. They would lift the truck to a set pressure on each corner and then make adjustments while driving down the road. These suffered from the same problems that occurred when using gauges and switches, but at least it was more automatic. AirLift Performance still uses this concept with its 3P system, although it has been greatly refined.

Then, height sensors were offered, and they changed the game. After these special linkage assemblies were installed to the suspension, it was now possible to dial in where the truck lifted and drove. With multiple presets available, the vehicle could be driven lowered one day and lifted the next—or the ride height could be changed to multiple positions all in one trip to the convenience store.

AccuAir dominated the market with its e-level kit, but AirLift Performance soon had the 3H, which also performed well. Today, other options are available from newcomers to the market, plus a few familiar faces. However, AccuAir and AirLift Performance are still the dominant brands.

These kits have another advantage too. Prior to their rise (pun intended), the debate when installing an air management system was around how fast a vehicle could be raised and lowered. These new digital air management systems make the decision obsolete. They move as fast as the system allows, and really, there's no hurry. Only a select few people care if the front wheels are hopping off the ground anymore.

Smaller lines, such as 1/4- and even 1/8-inch, can be used, which provides more space and easier components to work with. These systems also made airbags more popular among the general public and more accessible as a result. In fact, they've become so popular that most builders start with their decision of which digital air management system to use and go from there.

Is it right for you? Chances are good that your answer is yes. These setups are incredibly convenient, and they make the airbag experience much more pleasurable. Yes, mounting the sensors is more complex, and that makes things take more time. However, the result is worth it, so it's something to consider for your OBS truck.

Airbag Installation

Let's walk through an entire airbag installation from start to finish. In this case, the owner of this 1995 Chevrolet Silverado standard cab wanted to go from a 2/4 drop to laying on the frame and, eventually, the body. To do so, parts were used from Chris Alston's Chassisworks, KP Components, Slam Specialties, AVS, and Viair. Todd at Lowboy Motorsports in Mesa, Arizona, performed the installation.

Disassembling the Front Suspension

1 *With the truck on jack stands and the wheels removed, remove the front sway bar.*

2 *After removing the cotter pin, remove the spindle nut. Normally, the entire brake and spindle assembly can be removed as one. However, in this case, the truck needed dropped spindles to get low enough.*

Disassembling the Front Suspension *continued*

3 *With the lower control arm safely propped up by a jack, remove the front springs and set them aside. Then, unbolt the control arms to create space to work.*

Making Clearance for the Airbags

1 *Using a piece of scrap from a previous install as a template, Todd from Lowboy marks the area to cut on the frame.*

2 *The airbags need a significant amount of space. Otherwise, they won't allow the suspension to come up high enough to clear bigger wheels. In addition, watch out for the bags rubbing. Removing this section of the frame helps.*

3 *The easiest way to remove the metal is with a plasma cutter. However, a cut-off wheel or even a reciprocating saw will work in a pinch.*

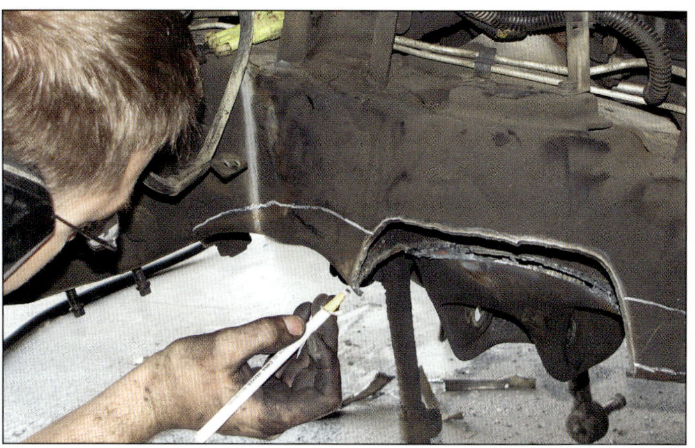

4 *The issue now is clearance for the tie-rod ends and the lower control arms. Todd marks the areas to remove with a grease pencil.*

Making Clearance for the Airbags *continued*

5 *This is what remains after everything is cut out. Admittedly, this may look scary, but don't worry. There's a plan.*

6 *Todd welds up the new holes using the factory metal. This creates space for the suspension and the airbag. He also ground down the lip of the frame by the bag so that it was smooth.*

Installing the Front Airbags

1 *The Slam Specialties bag is mounted to a top cup. This does a few things. First, it spaces the bag away from the top, providing clearance so that it does not rub. Second, it provides a spot for a threaded rod. This goes into the stock shock stem hole.*

2 *Install the KP Components control arms with the dropped spindle. The lower control arms have a mounting spot for the bottom of the bag so that it can be directly bolted in place.*

3 *With the brakes reinstalled, the front end is ready to go. If the owner wanted to install with bigger wheels (it's set up for 22s), the cup could be cut down to get more drop.*

4 *The front shock mounts needed trimming to match the notched frame. Then, they were bolted into place.*

Relocating Engine Bay Components

1 The wiring harness on the driver's side is in the way of the wheels, which means that it can rub. The solution is to cut out the mounting hole and relocate it to the side.

2 After the panel has been cut out, use it to make a template for a filler panel.

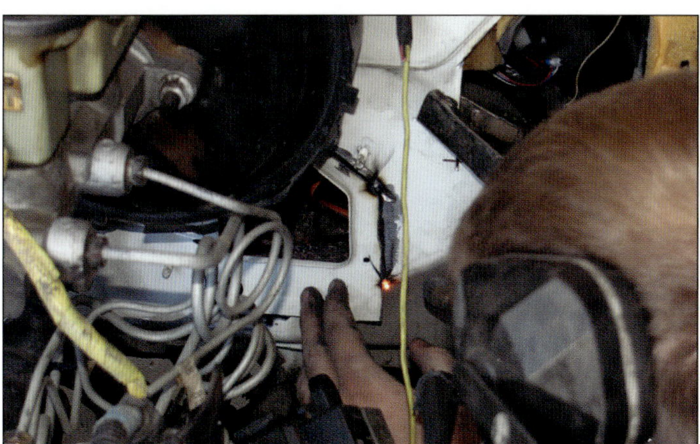

3 A new location has been chosen below the brake booster. It rotates the harness 90 degrees and keeps the wiring far away from the tires. The filler panel is tacked and then fully welded in place. Then, everything is painted to prevent rust.

4 A custom bracket that holds the fuse block and the ABS harness was created that mounts to the brake booster and the firewall.

5 The coolant overflow needed a new home as well. The stock one works in this scenario, but an aftermarket one can be used if you prefer.

Installing Fender Tubs

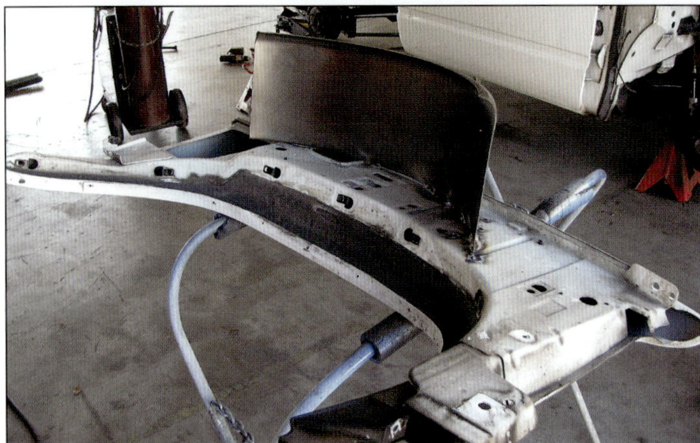

1 The wheels tuck into the fenders but hit the stock sheet metal. The solution is to install new inner fenders made from trailer parts. Begin by tacking them into place on the existing metal.

2 Using a cut-off wheel, carefully remove the metal around the new fender.

3 Tack the new fender into place. Now, the wheel has enough clearance.

4 The finishing touch is using a bit of seam sealer over the welds. This gives it a factory appearance and provides protection.

Disassembling the Rear Suspension

1 With the bed out of the way, it is possible to see what was on the truck originally: stock leaf springs and a welded-in C-notch. Unbolt the leaf springs and set them aside.

Disassembling the Rear Suspension *continued*

2 Remove the leaf-spring mounts. This involves cutting an "X" shape into the rivets with a cut-off wheel and then using an air hammer to knock off the heads.

3 The previous owner of this truck welded on the axle-flip kit, so it is being removed. The easiest way to do so is with a plasma cutter.

Installing the Rear Kit

1 The truck is getting a KP Components 6-link kit. To keep the axle centered, a Watt's link is used. To start the installation process, unbolt but do not remove the differential cover.

2 Mount the assembled Watt's link bracket to the axle with the provided hardware.

3 Bolt up the axle brackets. They are secured with U-bolts and slot into the existing leaf-spring saddles.

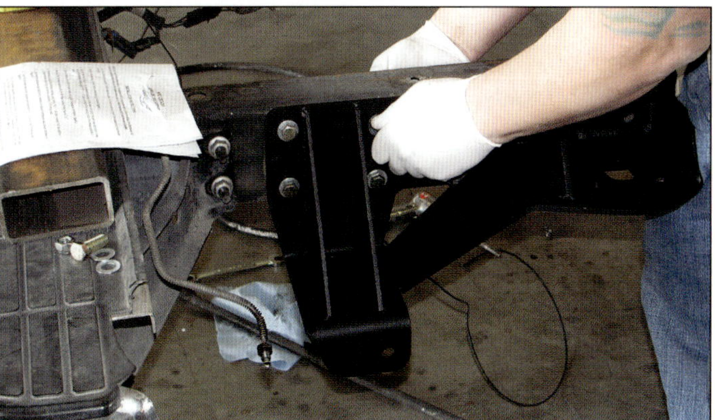

4 The aft brackets bolt into the stock hanger location, but they also need additional holes. To begin that process, bolt the mounts into place in the locations that were previously holding the hanger in place with rivets.

Installing the Rear Kit *continued*

5 *Use a center punch to mark the new hole locations on the frame. This is done on both sides, and then the brackets are removed.*

6 *Drill the holes using progressively larger bits.*

7 *Bolt in the back brackets for the last time, using the provided grade-8 hardware and Loctite.*

8 *The front mounts bolt into the factory leaf-spring-mount holes. These hold the parallel 4-link bars and keep the axle moving smoothly up and down in relation to the frame.*

Bridging the Frame

To get the rear of these trucks to sit on the frame, a bridge notch is needed. "Bridging" the frame requires installing one of these notches. It is possible to build a bridge notch using boxed tubing, or an 8-piece kit can be used, as is shown in this portion of the project.

1 *Determine where the lower part of the bridge notch should sit for the truck to lay on the frame. Then, position one of the side pieces of the eight-piece notch so that it is centered over the axle.*

Bridging the Frame *continued*

2 *With the inside piece welded in place, remove the old C-notch. This involves a lot of cutting, since it was welded in place.*

3 *After the old notch is out, assemble the rest of the kit and weld it into place.*

Making Air Management Mounts and Adjustments

1 *Todd fabricated new mounts in the back to hold the air tanks. Then, he used some prebuilt brackets for the compressors.*

2 *A problem that arose dealt with the driveline. It was too close to a crossmember, so it had to be notched as well.*

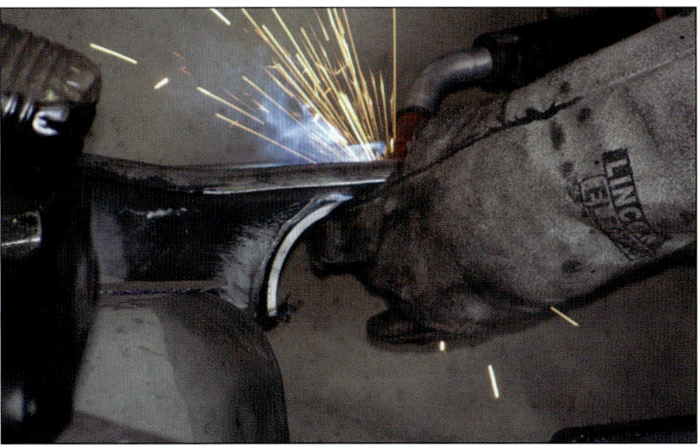

3 *Using a piece of pipe as a template, Todd cut out the crossmember using a plasma cutter. Then, he cut down and welded the pipe into place.*

Installing Air Management

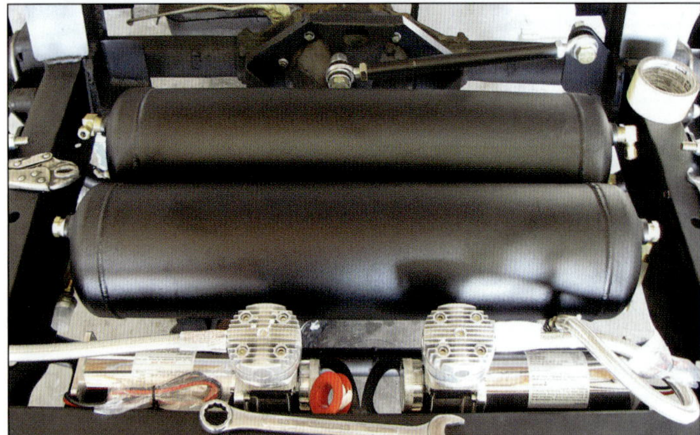

1 *In this build, the tanks and two Viair compressors were plumbed. Then, everything was wired up.*

2 *The valves are joined as one assembly. Each fitting presents an opportunity for leaks, and the whole thing took up a lot of space.*

3 *Barrier strips such as these make the wiring process a lot cleaner. If something needs to be adjusted or relocated later, it's simpler than it would be without a barrier strip.*

4 *Wire the compressors to a high-amperage relay such as this one. This is not only reliable but also a simple way to do both compressors off one unit.*

5 *The completed truck looks great laid out on 20-inch wheels. Now, it is time for a body drop.*

CHAPTER 7

ENGINES AND TRANSMISSIONS

The engine is the heart and soul of a truck. It motivates the vehicle to go down the road, and, when it is presented properly, popping the hood is like opening up a jewel box to present a shiny object inside. How an engine is built and presented is a big deal, particularly in the custom truck world. However, how do you know what route you need to take?

There are several options.

The first option is to go the stock route, which could mean using a stock replacement engine or upgrading to something larger. Maybe your truck has a 4.3L V-6, but you want a 454 big-block. Sure, that's one way to do it. However, another option is to use the 4.3L engine and add a twin-turbo setup. You can take what you already have to the next level.

Second, there are period-correct swaps. While it's not for everyone, it has its place. If you want something of the era, look at what the Corvette had at the time: the LT1. Those engines produced up to 300 hp, and because they're considered to be out of date, you can find one relatively affordably. Yes, it's not as powerful or advanced as the next few options, but it is what was done at the time. In addition, if you want something that's from the same era, it doesn't get much better than that.

The third option is an LS or LT engine swap. This is considered by many to be the ultimate engine upgrade for these trucks. For some, it's even considered to be a standard upgrade. In fact, when buying an aftermarket chassis for these trucks,

The owner of this truck decided to swap the original 5.7L Vortec V-8 with an LS3, which was dropped into his new chassis. (Photo Courtesy Lonnie Thompson)

That previously pictured LS3 can also be installed into a Tahoe. (Photo Courtesy Lonnie Thompson)

selecting LS or LT motor mounts is usually an option.

There's a lot to like about going this route. A brand-new crate engine from General Motors can be purchased with all of the goodies. In addition, some crazy builders offer drop-in kits with a supercharger and fully built bottom end. Going with a crate engine from the factory isn't bad because you know that you're getting exactly what you need.

The engine that you choose will shape the build of your truck as well as its drivability and the general fun factor when it is taken to a show. So, here (arguably more than in any other chapter), you must think about your budget.

As of this writing, Texas Speed & Performance, one of the more well-known engine builders in the country, offers various LSX packages that cost about $25,000 each. Not everyone has $25,000 to spend on a motor, particularly when the truck itself may have cost less than $5,000. Compare that to a replacement 350-ci V-8 for $4,000, and now you have to decide if the build is more important than the budget.

No matter what you do, getting a new engine for your truck is a big decision. To make the best decision possible, let's walk through the process.

Stock Engine Options

OBS trucks were available with a few different powertrain options. The one that is currently in your vehicle will shape your decision-making process.

Let's begin with the 4.3L V-6. Although it wasn't a popular model when it was released, there are fans of the motor today. It's essentially a 350-ci V-8 with two cylinders lopped off, and it's a pretty reliable setup. Some people love adding superchargers or turbos to beef it up. However, doing so isn't *that* popular. It's basically a niche market with its supporters, but it's not likely that you will bump into any of them at a local car meet. For the purposes of this book, just assume that a 4.3L V-6 will be upgraded to a V-8. If not, there are many places that can help you out.

The next option is a 305-ci V-8. Its main selling point is better gas mileage. Visually, there aren't many ways to tell the difference between a 305 and a 350 engine when they are shown at a car show. If they are dressed up with nice parts, no one really cares. So, if you just want to rebuild the 305 to clean up the engine, that's not a bad plan. Now, if you want to build a 1,000-hp monster, then this isn't the starting point for you. However, if the goal is to just use something that can be cleaned up and made to look good, consider this option.

Next is the 350-ci V-8, which many people consider to be the standard starting point for these trucks. It's a reliable engine with many performance modifications that are available to the general public. The bonus is that if something breaks, you're an AutoZone or O'Reilly's Auto Parts away from getting it fixed with parts that are on the shelf. Heck, if the engine throws a rod, a new one can be found at those same shops, usually the same day. Seriously, these things are everywhere.

That's not to say that you must get a 350—far from it. However, it is accessible and approachable from a price perspective too. If you just want to keep your stuff simple, a 350 engine is a good option.

Period-Correct Swaps

Engine experts say the LT-1 that was originally produced from 1970 to 1972 was really just a 350-ci V-8 that was found in Camaros and Corvettes from the time. However, to those who grew up or had their formidable years in the 1990s, then the LT1 (no hyphen) was a whole other thing.

Chevy built the LT1 from 1992 to 1997, and it was offered in the Corvette and the rare 1994–1996 Impala SS. These engines were created as a tribute to the original LT-1 but had 300 hp and 340 ft-lbs of torque. These were truly popular engines, and if it wasn't for the introduction of the LS line, they may have continued to be in production for years.

This Tahoe has a 5.7L Vortec V-8, which was standard in the two-door SUVs. (Photo Courtesy Lonnie Thompson)

If you're paying attention to the LT1's year range (1992 to 1997), you'll notice that it's smack dab in the middle of the OBS era. Therefore, it is a perfect period-correct swap. As you probably expected, this was a common swap in the 1990s. There were OBS trucks with LT1s at shows across the nation, so doing it today is certainly not a bad idea.

The issue is availability. A crate engine can be purchased from Jegs for less than $2,800, but it will still need the intake manifold and the front drive parts. Otherwise, you can go junkyard hunting to get exactly what you want. What makes things worse is that the next-gen LS engine is known as the LT-1 (with the hyphen) too, which makes a Google search even more difficult.

This is not meant to discourage you in your hunt for the ideal motor—far from it. Have some fun junkyard diving for parts and pick up something inexpensive that can be rebuilt. There are many opportunities for the right period-correct motor for your truck. You just need to do some hunting to get there.

This stepside is stuffed with an LT1 engine from a Corvette. It looks good in the engine bay and performs well.

There's nothing wrong with getting an LS3 crate motor and transmission for your build—aside from the price. (Photo Courtesy Lonnie Thompson)

LS and LT Swaps

The aim of this book is not to explain every detail of the installation process of an LS or LT engine. Fortunately, a book already exists that does just that: *How to Swap LS & LT Engines Into Chevy & GMC Trucks: 1960–1998* by Jefferson Bryant. Bryant gets into the minutiae of how these swaps work. For example, here's one quote: "The 1997–1998 LS1 wire harness is different from the 1999–2002 models, and the Vortec truck harnesses are different from those."

It sounds like getting the wiring figured out will be a whole lot of fun.

This is an LS Gen 4 engine, and it was what Ruben wanted for his Tahoe build. It's reliable and can produce a lot of power, but not so much as to make it unreliable. (Photo Courtesy Ruben Castañon)

That is, unless you get the correct guidance. Bryant's book has all of the details needed to do a swap correctly, so go to cartechbooks.com to pick up your copy.

With that being said, there are still many things to discuss. The LS came in Gen III and Gen IV versions, while the LT is a Gen V. The engine that you select should be based on several factors, including price and availability. Do you want to buy something from a junkyard or brand new from the dealer? How much horsepower do you want to make?

It's easy to say, "I want an LS engine," and then buy whatever flavor you prefer—maybe an LSX or LS3. However, first consider some other questions and use your answers to make your decisions for the rest of the build.

For example, if you want to build a cruiser, does it need a supercharged LT5? Probably not. A junkyard LQ9 may do just as well and still get some looks at the local show. However, if you're building your truck for drag racing, that LT5 might be just the start—assuming that you have the money.

Again, this book addresses the broad strokes to consider before performing an engine swap, assuming that you want one.

To get everything from Point A to Point B, the easiest way is to convert all connections to AN lines. This is a collection of parts that are used in the process. (Photo Courtesy Ruben Castañon)

Fuel Delivery

At some point, gas needs to get to the engine. If you're going from a Vortec V-8 to an LS, some changes must be made.

That begins with installing a new fuel pump into the original tank and then figuring out how to get the fuel delivered.

Electric Fans

An issue that can occur during an engine swap deals with the original cooling fan. It often doesn't fit in the

This is the fuel pump and sender that will be installed in the tank. (Photo Courtesy Ruben Castañon)

To keep things looking as factory as possible, Ruben kept a lot of his factory shroud in place, even though it wasn't entirely necessary. (Photo Courtesy Ruben Castañon)

The fans fit nicely and are still a bit stealthy. (Photo Courtesy Ruben Castañon)

factory shroud. The easy solution is to convert to electric fans. These turn on only when necessary and still provide adequate cooling.

Accelerator Pedal

The newer engines run on a drive-by-wire system, meaning that there is no mechanical linkage going from the accelerator pedal to the throttle body. Instead, the pedal has to be wired into the system.

Engine Upgrades

Many things can be done to these trucks, and whether working on a brand-new LSX or an older 5.7L engine, some of them are fairly universal. That's where things get interesting.

An engine runs on fuel, spark, and air. With newer engines, a laptop can be connected and used to adjust the ratios of each and where they go. However, with an older engine, some fun things can still be done. In both cases, each component needs to be tweaked to better serve your purposes.

Let's start with air. One way to gain horsepower is to improve the airflow that's going into and coming out of the engine. The idea is to reduce restrictions. This is why it is best for an exhaust to have minimal turns and no kinks, like a factory exhaust might have. It's also a reason to upgrade things such as exhaust manifolds, which are often called "headers." They give the air a smoother pathway to exit.

The same idea applies to the air intake. With a less-restrictive filter and tubing, the air will enter the engine faster, which provides increased horsepower.

Turbochargers and superchargers are on the extreme end of the spec-

This is the new drive-by-wire pedal placed on top of the stock pedal for comparison. It will land in more or less the same place from the foot's perspective, but it will sit a little bit differently on the firewall. (Photo Courtesy Ruben Castañon)

These headers will be installed on a 2008-plus Gen IV LS engine. They dramatically improve the exhaust airflow. (Photo Courtesy Ruben Castañon)

Whether the harness was built by you or premade, properly label the wiring. (Photo Courtesy Ruben Castañon)

Part of the way that these headers improve exhaust airflow is by removing restrictions. Here, where all four tubes meet, the steel comes to a point, allowing airflow to move quickly. (Photo Courtesy Ruben Castañon)

trum. They provide more air to the engine by using different methods. A turbo system uses exhaust gases to spin the turbo, which then sends more air into the engine. A supercharger does the same thing, but it is driven by a belt system instead of exhaust gases.

In both cases, it's important to adjust the air/fuel ratio. That's where new fuel injectors and/or computer tuning come into play. These are more complex ways to improve horsepower for sure, but they definitely can increase the numbers.

From there, it's about building the engine to handle the boost and added pressure. The valves, pistons, heads, etc. work together to help the engine stay in one piece. It's not always easy, and it's definitely not cheap. However, the point is that there are some options with forced induction to push 1,000 hp with an OBS truck.

Transmission Options

Several transmission options were available with these trucks. Some could get a 5-speed manual, but for the most part, column-shifted automatics were offered.

Most trucks were automatics, and they were likely a 700R4, a 4L60, or a 4L60E. Often, particularly with the original models, the transmission type can be determined by the shape of the transmission pan.

The question ultimately comes down to what you want to do with your truck. When looking for a reliable cruiser, the 4L60 transmissions perform well. However, if you want something beefier to handle more power with a period-correct engine, the 4L80 would work well.

On the LS/LT front, you would've been looking at 4L60s, but now it's the 4L60E. It is possible, of course, to go with a Tremec 5- or 6-speed, if that was desired, but the 4L60Es do just fine and can handle a decent amount of power.

Whatever you do to beef up the engine, make sure that the transmission can handle the power increase. There's nothing worse than grenading a transmission after you've finally worked all of the kinks out of the engine.

Transmission Options

Manual	Automatic
NV3500	THM400
NV4500	700R4
HM290	4L60
5LM60	4L60E
	4L80E

The shape of this particular pan makes this transmission either a 700R4 or a 4L60 transmission. But knowing that it's the original setup, and that the truck is a 1998 Tahoe, it's more likely a 4L60.

Body and Paint

If there is one aspect that shapes the way that a truck is viewed, it's the paint. No decision is more consequential. It's also one of the most expensive parts of the project.

The paint is the first thing that anyone sees when they walk up to a vehicle. Does it have scratches, chips, or dings? Is the truck straight or wavy like potato chips? Can a reflection be seen in the shine or is it cloudy and hazy? Unless the goal is to have a patina look (and there's nothing wrong with that), paint can make or break your ride.

The problem for most people is the cost. A good paint job is not inexpensive, and an inexpensive paint job is usually not good. There's a balance. In the end, you're determining what you can afford versus the standard that you want to set for your ride.

The bodywork takes things up another notch too. If you're going for a basic restomod look for the outside, maybe don't remove things such as the door handles, tailgate handle, or bed stake pockets. It's important to get the body straight enough that it looks good. If you do want to shave some parts or do custom work, it gets expensive. Even just adding a roll pan to the truck will increase the price and complexity—and that's a period-correct modification that most people want to do.

The purpose of this discussion was not meant to deter you from building the truck that you want. Instead, it is in this book to make you aware of the consequences of your actions. It is easy to find yourself at $30,000 on paint and bodywork, and that's a tough bill to swallow. Know what you're getting into and what you can afford. Then, find the people who can help to make it happen.

While this book doesn't go down the rabbit hole that is everything that custom paint involves, it covers the aspects that are important for OBS owners to know.

This may look like a simple paint job, but it wasn't. Black trucks need bodywork that has been well done. Otherwise, everything looks wavy.

Custom Modifications

From a custom modification perspective, there are many options for OBS trucks. The categories are below.

Bolt-On Modifications

The first and most obvious type of modification is a bolt-on. The idea is that this is a modification that can "bolt on" to change a truck. The other key part of that statement is that you could also eventually unbolt it, if you want to go back to the stock configuration. These modifications don't require actual nuts and bolts as long as they can be removed safely in the future.

Many things fall into this category, including bumpers, grilles, hoods, third brake lights, taillights, adhesive moldings, and some body kits. If it goes on but can be pulled off, it's a bolt-on modification.

You may have noticed that hoods were part of the list. Although they do bolt on and off, they also require paint (unless they're carbon fiber). While that is true, the same rule applies. If the old hood is kept, it can always be swapped out.

Suspension also falls into this category, with the exception of C-notches, bridges, and any weld-on components. These are obviously not bolt-ons because they aren't easily removable.

This may sound tricky, as some C-notches technically do bolt in. However, a bolt-on modification is more about being able to return the truck back to the stock configuration. The frame has to be cut to install a C-notch, so returning the frame to its original condition is not possible.

If you live in an area that doesn't get a lot of rain or if the truck is mainly built for show, then these modifications are for you. They clean up the look of the front of a truck and remove the clutter on the windshield.

Installing Billet Wiper Caps

1 The first step is to remove the old wipers from the truck. There's a little tab at the base that locks each wiper to the motor. Use a flathead screwdriver to open it up.

2 It may take some work to pull the arm off the motor. Note the protruding keyway. You will need to know its location shortly.

3 Look inside the LG Billet wiper post cover to look for two things: 1) a spring that helps retain pressure on the mount so that it doesn't need any mounting hardware and 2) a smooth portion (seen on the right in this photo).

4 Using that smooth portion as a guide, align it with the keyway. Then, push down and twist to lock the billet part in place. It can be removed in the opposite way if it rains so that it can be replaced with working wipers.

This particular truck has several weld-on modifications, including shaved door handles, a suicide hood, a frenched front license plate, shaved stake pockets, and shaved bed rails. (Photo Courtesy Ruben Castañon)

Weld-On Modifications

Weld-on modifications require something to be welded onto the truck or affixed permanently.

Many items in this category are suspension related. Bridges and C-notches are common modifications in this category, but so are a lot of link suspensions as well as most air suspension systems.

However, this is the paint and body chapter, and that means weld-on modifications include roll pans, shaved accessories, and extensive bodywork. A popular example of this deals with the bumpers. Some folks like to narrow the front and/or rear bumper so that the sides are flush with the fenders. They may even push everything inward so that the front end is more or less flat.

This kind of modification involves a substantial amount of welding, but the result is pretty slick when done right. You definitely have to work the bumper brackets to make this happen and maybe even modify the frame itself, depending on your approach.

Regardless, if a modification requires welding, it's a weld-on modification.

Roll Pans

When building a period-correct custom truck, consider a roll pan. These are rear bumper replacements that connect the two bed sides together, rolling down and smoothing out the rear of the truck. These were massively popular in the 1990s, and they are almost considered a standard part today.

There are multiple options for a roll pan. Bolt-on roll pans are what they sound like because they bolt onto the truck. Typically, there is a row of screws that are installed underneath the tailgate and in the lower part of the bed. Then, the sides are secured to the bed sides. This leaves a seam but provides the basic overall look.

For a smoother appearance, weld in the pan. Almost all of the same rules apply here, but this modification replaces the bolts and screws with welding. The main difference is the connection to the bed sides. With welding, the outer sheet metal joins together so that it creates a seamless look after the appropriate bodywork has been performed. Personal opinions are obviously subjective, but this is usually considered to be a better way to do the modification, as it ties everything together nicely.

Roll pans are available in various materials. The cheaper option is fiberglass, which has all of the problems that are inherent with that material. It's not very flexible, and fitment can be challenging. However, if it is done correctly, it should be okay. In addition, it can be tweaked if you're handy with fiberglass.

This is a weld-in roll pan on a Chevy Tahoe. Note how tight the gaps are and how clean it looks blended in. That's the goal. (Photo Courtesy Ruben Castañon)

The next choice is urethane or other plastics. These are exceedingly rare but are available from Street Scene. These are usually better than fiberglass, and they are definitely able to take more of an impact. However, you're limited to getting what is provided, as modifying the plastic is not impossible but usually not worth it for the time and effort.

Finally, steel roll pans are available as bolt-on and weld-on models. It is possible to buy a blank model and weld in everything that you like—from taillights to billet inserts or anything else. Some shops, such as GrantFab, offer many variations, meaning that you can make yours truly custom, such as if it has a license plate box or not.

While it might seem obvious when replacing the bumper to have a place to put a license plate, that doesn't mean the plate *needs* to be in the new roll pan. It depends on the laws in your state, but some builders have become really creative. They'll weld on a smooth roll pan and have a plate that hinges down underneath the pan itself. Otherwise, they'll add a bracket that connects to the tailgate or even weld a box into it. It's up to you, your creativity, and the laws in your state.

This is an all-metal roll pan, complete with a license-plate box. (Photo Courtesy Ruben Castañon)

Shaving Door Handles and More

When something is "shaved," that means the part was taken off, the hole where it previously was has been welded up, and bodywork was performed so that no one can tell that it was there in the first place. For example, shaved door handles require removing the door handles, welding in a plate, performing bodywork to make it flush, and then finishing it with paint. Voila, the handle was never there.

Many parts can be shaved on OBS trucks, including the taillights, door handles, stake pockets, antennas, tailgate handles, and gas doors. There are a wide variety of reasons to shave parts. In the case of the door handles, these trucks have a pretty big security flaw if the thief doesn't care about the bodywork. The door handle can be removed with a few quick pries, allowing a would-be crook to gain access to the interior of the truck. Shaving the door handles eliminates that problem, but it also presents a new one.

Something to consider when shaving a part from a truck is what will replace it after it has been removed. After all, you need to get inside the truck, so shaving the handles means that you need to figure out how to open the door. Shaving the taillights means finding new taillights to go somewhere.

Solutions exist for all of these problems, and you're building a custom truck, which requires custom solutions. Builders have been shaving door handles for decades. Determine which method you want to use. (For the record, heavy-duty solenoids pulling on the latch help, but the best option is having a stopper on a spring to push the door open when the latch engages. That's the hot ticket to making sure that things consistently work correctly.)

While shaving various pieces makes the build better, it also adds expense. All of that welding requires bodywork, which means paint as well. That's not a small amount of money, depending on how things are approached. To keep the truck the stock color, consider doing the modifications in zones. It is possible to remove the bed, weld up the taillights, and then work some magic with the paint to achieve the result that you want. The truck will temporarily look weird, but if the match is good, you'll get something cool in the end. The same goes with the opposite side of the truck, and both can reduce overall downtime.

Mirrors

Most states require a sideview mirror on a truck, usually at least one on the driver's side. These trucks came in many different models, and the mirror aftermarket is huge.

Some of the lower-model trucks came with huge elephant-ear mirrors that bolted to the door itself. Otherwise, the mirrors sat in the corners by the windows. Smaller sport-model mirrors are found on the 454 SS and similar versions. There's a sporty option from Street Scene, and even some with integrated turn signals. Another option is to go completely custom and get billet mirrors from a motorcycle. They're not as helpful from a driving perspective, but they look cool.

Front-End Conversions

A few different front ends were available for 1988–1998 Chevy and GMC trucks, but they weren't significantly different. Early models had quad headlights instead of single sealed-beam units, but that was the only major change that would require modifying the mounting brackets. Otherwise, swapping a grille from a Chevy to a GMC was pretty easy and could be done in an afternoon.

What was more difficult was a GMC Denali or Cadillac Escalade front clip. Those required more parts and were more expensive. In addition, the bumper sits on the ground, whereas the rest of the truck is on the frame. While the front bumper can be modified or replaced to accommodate a body drop, it is more difficult and time-consuming as a result.

The most popular front-clip modification involves converting the older 1988–1993 front ends to the more modern 1994-and-newer Chevrolet and GMC grilles. The installation is straightforward. It requires nothing more than a new grille and some time, with the possible exception of new corner lenses—assuming that the grille doesn't have them already.

Converting a Chevrolet Front End to a GMC

In this case, the project truck (a 1997 Chevrolet Silverado) had an aftermarket Chevrolet grille. It didn't fit properly, the badge was incorrect, and it looked horrible. After a search, the owner found a GMC grille in white that served his purposes. It just needed a little bit of work to make it happen.

Although it's more difficult to modify an Escalade's front bumper, it's possible. It can be done by plastic welding the stock piece or buying/building a fiberglass replacement.

The "original" grille wasn't in good shape. In addition, a close inspection of the bowtie shows that it wasn't an officially licensed grille, either.

This shows that the grille wasn't flush with the fender.

The grille was broken as well. This truck spent a lot of time in California, and while it's dry there—which is great for rust prevention—it's not great for plastic. The grille dry-rotted and broke.

Removing the Front Grille

1 To remove the grille, begin by removing the four screws that secure the marker lenses to the plastic. They come off with the grille, but it's easier to do it at this stage in the process.

2 Two bulbs are on the backside of the housing. Push and twist to remove them.

3 A 7-mm bolt is just above the badge area in the center of the grille. Use an extension on a ratchet to remove it.

4 The remaining screws on the top of the grille require a Phillips-head screwdriver.

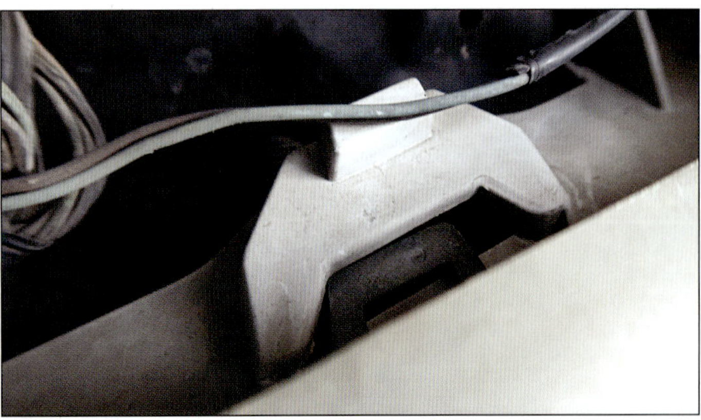

5 The bottom of the grille holds to another plastic trim piece with these clips. They're fragile, so lift up on them delicately so that they don't break.

6 With the grille free, the two light bulbs that are left are visible. Untwist the bulbs from the side-marker lenses by hand.

Replacing the Front Headlights

1 It may not be apparent in the picture, but these headlights have seen better days. They will be replaced with a new model that looks stock.

2 The headlights are attached with 10-mm bolts. A ratchet and an extension are needed to reach some of them.

3 One of the problems with the headlights was this aftermarket high-intensity discharge (HID) kit. It didn't work properly, built up too much heat, and flickered. Fortunately, removing the kit was easy because it used the factory harnesses.

4 These are Philips 9005 X-tremeVision bulbs (part number 9005XVB2), and they're being used for the inside bulbs. They twisted into the new headlights, which are a Spyder Auto model (part number HD-YD-CCK88-C).

5 The other bulbs are Philips 9006 VisionPlus (part number 9006VPB2). Install them the same way. Between the headlights and the bulbs, the cost was about $175 at Amazon. After assembling the lights, reinstall them onto the core support in the reverse order of disassembly.

Repairing the GMC Grille

1 There were signs of cracking on some of the mounting tabs.

2 This wasn't the only place, either. The center hole was also dangerously close to coming out completely.

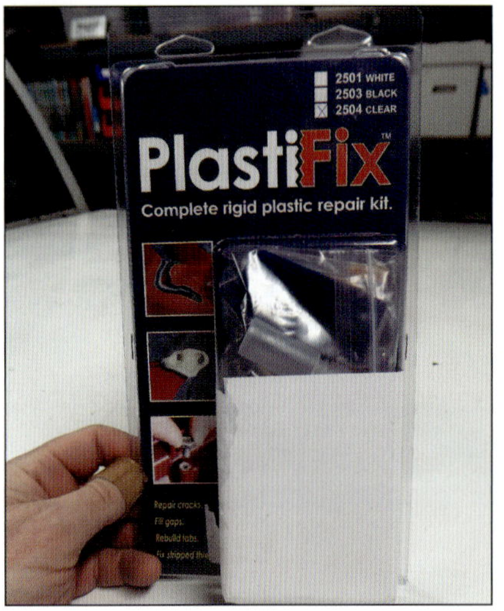

3 To fix the cracks, a Urethane Supply PlastiFix Kit from Amazon was purchased for about $50. This not only provided a way to fix the cracks in the plastic but also to replace damaged plastic in other locations.

4 First, grind out the existing cracks. Then, make a V-shaped groove over them with Dremel tool attachment number 121.

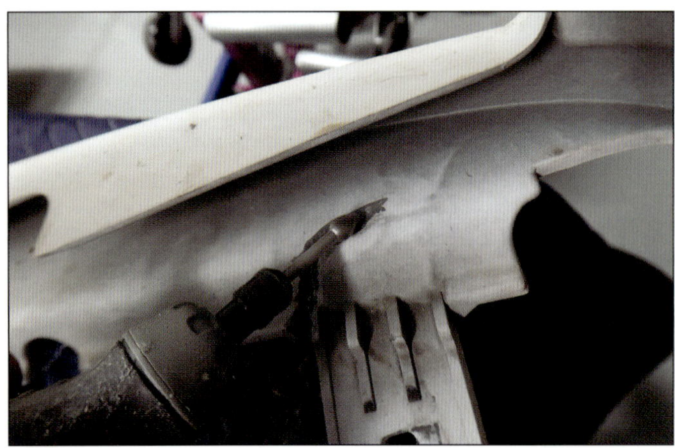

5 Use the tool to grind a shallow groove into the plastic. Don't go through the plastic, just give yourself a space to fill.

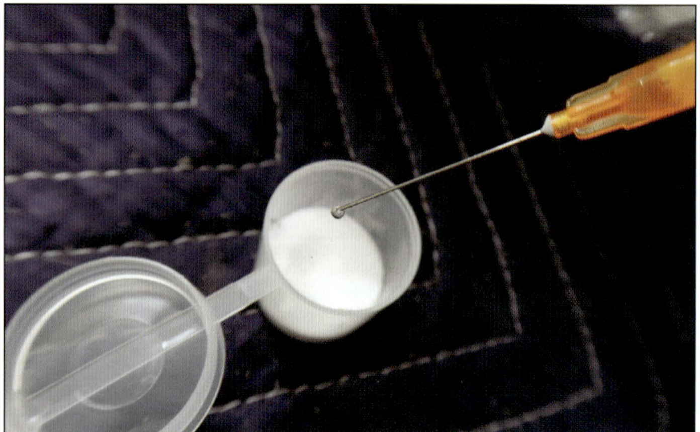

6 The kit uses a syringe and a powdered compound for the repairs. First, place a drop or two of the liquid into the powder.

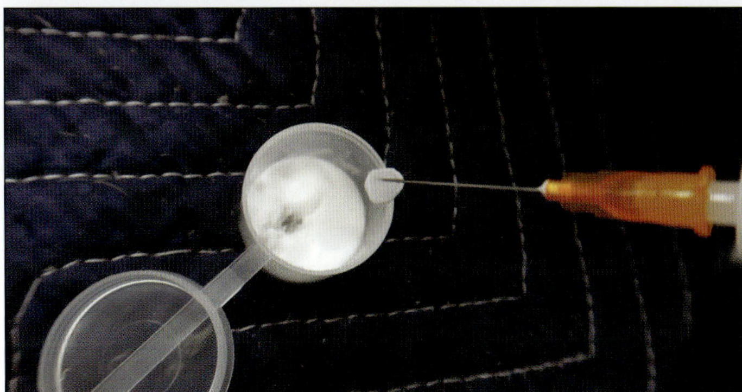

7 Now, use the syringe to pick up the plastic ball that's formed in the powder.

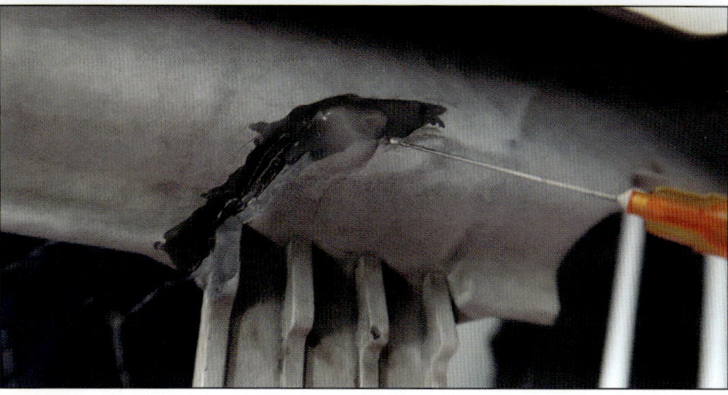

8 Place that ball onto the area that was ground down. Then, use a little bit of the liquid to melt it into the channel. It'll dry soon, providing new plastic to work with.

9 The center mount has several cracks. Grinding those holes would pop out the center piece. The solution is to make a mold using the materials in the kit.

10 After heating up some water, dump the molding material into the liquid to loosen it. The objective is to make it pliable enough to shape around the existing hole. Then, let it cool down and set it into place.

11 After letting the molding material cool down, a new end piece for the mount (or at least the basis for one) has been created.

12 With the brittle plastic removed, it is visible how the new part will work from the other side.

Repairing the GMC Grille *continued*

13 *Use the same syringe and powder method from before to create a new part.*

14 *With the mold material removed, set the new plastic into place. Once the center hole is cleaned up with the Dremel tool, it'll be ready for test fitting, primer, and paint.*

Installing a Billet Grille

We didn't want to just install a stock grille. Instead, the owner bought a T-Rex billet grille for about $210.

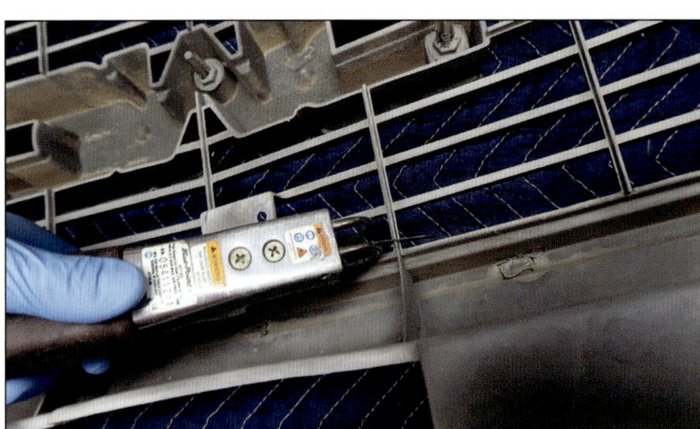

1 *The center insert on the grille needs to be removed, and a pneumatic saw does the job nicely. This gets the bulk of the center out of the way, but more fine tuning is required.*

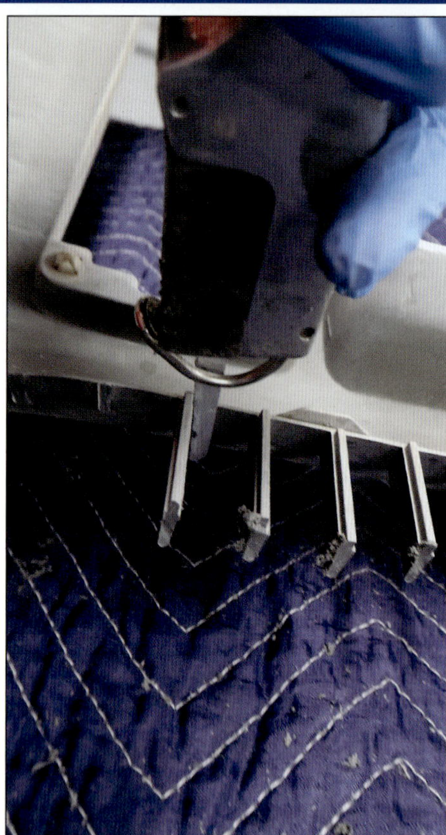

2 *Now it's time to take things closer, closing the gap. Ideally, the cut is flush but doesn't cut into the surrounding plastic.*

3 *There are vertical mounts for the grille that will rivet into the top of the plastic. For them to fit properly, the plastic surround has to be notched where the insert sat previously. Here, everything is marked out so that the cuts go smoothly.*

Installing a Billet Grille *continued*

4 *The cut itself doesn't need to be deep. It just needs to be enough for the billet grille to sit flush inside of the opening.*

5 *Place tape on the chrome trim to protect it for the next few steps, which involve sanding and painting.*

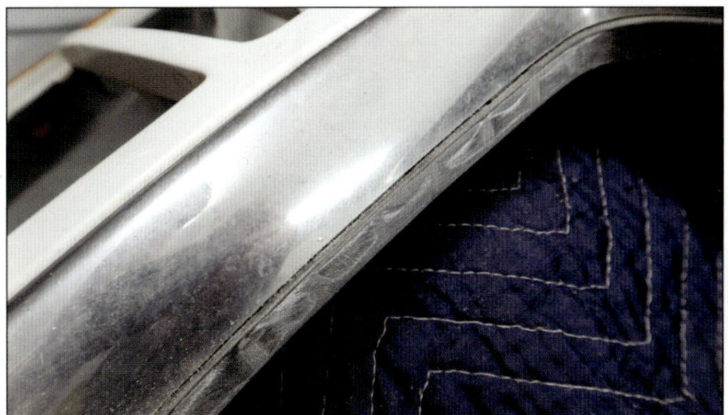

6 *Carefully sand the black plastic with an 80-grit sanding block to make everything smooth.*

7 *The grille is now set inside the opening and the lower mounts are drilled in place.*

8 *Use a piece of tape to mark the inside of the upper part of the grille for drilling. Mark the tape with a permanent marker and then drill.*

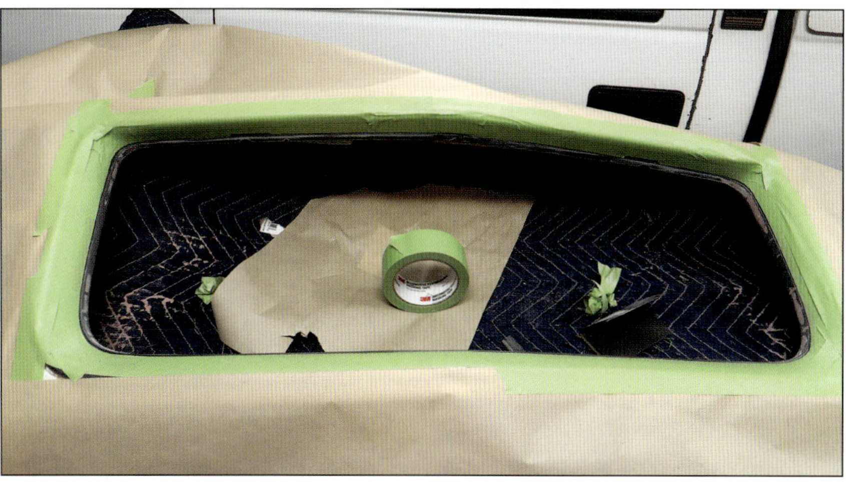

9 *With the billet insert out of the grille, mask and tape everything else. The black plastic portion of the GMC shell needed some bodywork. Then, it was painted black to match the original finish.*

Installing a Billet Grille *continued*

10 *After everything has dried, install the billet insert for the final time back into the shell. This requires using rivets that are pushed into place and then riveted.*

11 *Note that the billet insert doesn't work with the stock horn in its original location. Either remove the horn or relocate it behind the bumper.*

12 *The headlights need to be adjusted, but otherwise the grille is good to go.*

Removing Moldings

These trucks were built from 1988 to 1998, which makes them of a time when bodyside moldings were everywhere. If you own one of these trucks, chances are good that it has body side moldings too. They're ubiquitous with Silverados, and even lower-end models have the chrome fender trim.

One way to make a truck look worlds better is to remove the side moldings. On older Chevy and GMC trucks, that required special tools and welding up a bunch of holes. However, OBS truck

The body on this 1998 Chevrolet Tahoe is pretty straight, but the moldings need to be removed.

moldings were attached with double-sided tape. So, removing the trim is pretty straightforward, even on a truck that's more than 30 years old.

There are a few things to point out before going out into the garage and tearing off parts. First, be aware that removing trim will reveal paint that may have never seen the light of day. It may be brighter and/or more colorful than the rest of the panel because it hasn't faded. In addition, if the truck was ever in an accident, the paint underneath may not look good, as a shop at some point may have covered up damage with the molding. There could also be a dent or two underneath or even flaking paint if the trim was applied prematurely.

None of this matters if the truck will be repainted. However, if the goal is to make your daily driver look a bit better, be wary of what you may find.

Removing Body Side Moldings

1 *The chrome on the body trim of this 1998 Tahoe is rusting, and the chrome trim around the fenders doesn't look great, either.*

2 *There are several ways to get behind the moldings to remove them. Quite often, it is possible to just use your hands. In this case, a plastic squeegee was the best option.*

3 *Once you can grab onto it with your hands, do so. Then, just pull it back and off the truck.*

4 *The 3M double-sided tape remains. Rubbing it off by hand will tear up your fingers. Keep reading for a better way to remove it.*

Removing Double-Sided Tape

1 Clean the panel with a microfiber towel and some quick detailer. There will be dirt in the area where the molding was. Don't damage the paint further by grinding grime into the finish.

2 This is a 3M Adhesive Removal wheel. It costs about $55 on Amazon. These are great for removing old stickers, whether it's a hood stripe or double-sided tape.

3 Put the eraser wheel into a drill. Then, put the side of the eraser wheel against the adhesive that you want to remove. It's mostly a two-handed operation. Play around with various speeds to find the right setting for your project.

4 This is what you'll end up with. Notice that the ends of the top strip of adhesive have been completely removed, while the middle needs some more work.

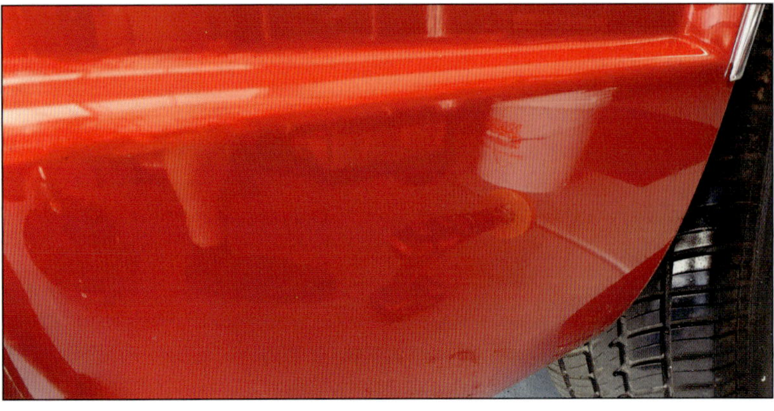

5 After both stripes are done and the panel has been rubbed with some quick detailer and a microfiber towel, this is the result. It looks perfect.

Removing Fender Trim

1 The chrome fender trim can be left on if you want. If you prefer a cleaner look, they're easy to remove. Just unbolt the 8-mm bolts that hold them to the body.

2 When removing them, be careful to avoid scratching the paint. Removing the top bolts last can help.

3 A microfiber towel and some quick detailer takes care of the leftover dirt.

Discoveries and Cover Ups

1 This is what the paint looked like under the passenger-side moldings. It is bubbled and flakey, and there are a few pinholes. It's not noticeable from 5 feet away, but it needs to be fixed at some point.

2 The passenger-side fender trim was covering up some nasty flaws. There were several dents and paint chips.

Discoveries and Cover Ups *continued*

3 *The previous owners cut and rolled the inner fenders for tire clearance but didn't do a good job. The truck will eventually get painted, so it's okay. However, if the plan was to leave it as is, the fender would need to get fixed or replaced.*

4 *Aside from the mess behind the moldings and trim, the resulting job looks good. After the bumper is swapped out with one that doesn't have the moldings, it will look better.*

Graphics

If racing stripes, tribal patterns, or flames are painted on the truck, then it has some variation of graphics. It's the ultimate modification to a paint job, and it is usually the last one that people do.

Think of graphics like a tattoo for a truck. Not everyone will like it, but it's your vehicle, so you can do what you want. In addition, consider the artist. He or she has a vision too, and whatever he or she thinks is best to create should be considered in the process. Sometimes, what we want may *sound* good, but it would look horrible in practice.

In the 1990s, there were a lot of variations of the flame paint job. This is where flames appear to run down the side of the truck, usually starting at the hood and working toward the back. There are hot rod flames, which look like what is seen at any street rodder show across the country. Real flames take that concept and make it more realistic. Reverse flames use the base color as the flame pattern and then do something wild for the rest of the body.

Tribal patterns were popular in the 1980s and 1990s, and they are making a comeback today. These are wild designs with various elements. Kal Koncepts is a shop that was big in this space at the time and remains that way today.

The sky's the limit. Do a mural of your dog on the tailgate or make the hood look like it's made of bones. Graphics are a unique form of your expression, so have at it.

Wraps

In recent years, vinyl wraps have significantly changed the custom car and truck scene. This is when a special vinyl material (similar to a giant sticker) is applied over the surface of the truck. If you've ever seen an A/C repair guy's truck, you've probably seen a wrap.

Today's vinyl can get pretty high end, and that means they can perform really well in different temperatures and conditions. Thousands of color and finish options are available, and a custom design is pretty easy too. Some people even install the wrap themselves.

There is also some controversy around the subject, though. Some call wraps cheating or think it's a shortcut around a "real" paint job. The appeal of a wrap is that it's usually cheaper than paint, but the more complex and high-end the vinyl is, the more the line blurs.

Regardless, if you are considering using a vinyl wrap, make sure the bodywork has been completed first and done well. Wraps don't hide much if anything, so all of those waves and defects in a truck's body will shine through. In addition, a vehicle can't just be wrapped with bare filler because it's not a rust protectant. Either way, the truck needs to have primer on it at a minimum to be safe from rust, and even that isn't always enough. So really, you may not save as much money as you think if you decide to go this route.

Pinstriping

The popularity of pinstriping comes and goes. It's a traditional hot rod look that appeals to an older generation, but younger folks like the way they can get super creative with the lines. It's pretty hard to knock a good pinstriping job.

There are many ways to pinstripe a truck. Some people freehand their designs, while others intricately mask and mark off the hood to follow a pattern. In the project truck shown here, the pinstriper used the latter technique to create a two-tone design that worked with the truck's color scheme.

Pinstriping

1 *Degrease the hood to eliminate any surface contaminants so that the paint can adhere properly.*

2 *Using blue fine-line tape, lay out a centerline for the hood to use as the basis of the design.*

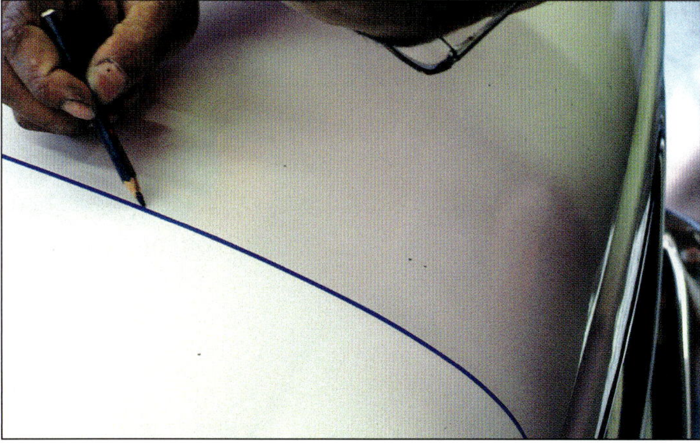

3 *Mark the line with a Stabilo pen. This can be removed easily from the paint, but it can be used as a guide that you can paint over.*

4 *Do the same thing on the horizontal axis. Lay down the tape, make marks with a Stabilo pen, and remove the tape.*

5 *By laying down a 1.5-inch-wide strip of masking tape parallel to the horizontal line, a pattern can be created up the hood. Do the same process with lines in a perpendicular direction.*

6 *The result is a grid of Stabilo pen marks that can be used as a reference for a design that was created previously on paper.*

Pinstriping *continued*

7 *Using the grid and design as a guide, lay out the pattern onto the hood using a Stabilo pen. Now, trace the lines using a pinstriping brush, which is not easy and requires a steady hand.*

8 *Prepare all of the brushes, reducers, and tape on a nearby table. In this case, OneShot pinstriping paint that has been slightly reduced is used for a smooth flow.*

9 *Apply a mix of paint and reducer to the paper using a technique called "loading the brush." The idea is to get the paint to flow at a consistency that will allow the artist to pull a line for a long distance.*

10 *Each line is laid down by using a finger or two to stabilize your hand, jamming the end of the brush into the webbing between your index finger and thumb, and making a long movement.*

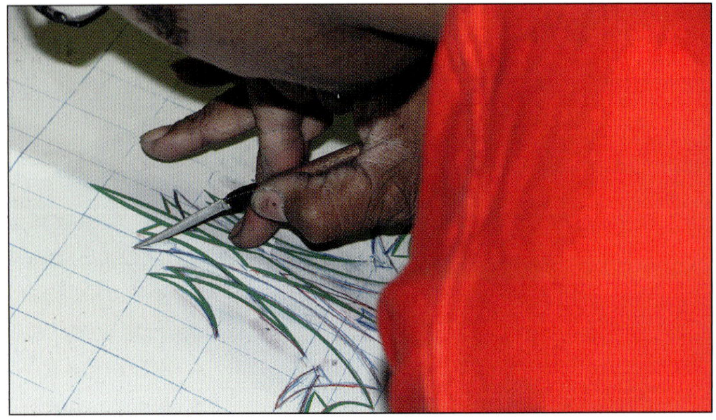

11 *Work on the art until it's time to switch colors. Then, use the same technique. In this case, the artist uses silver around the green to give it depth.*

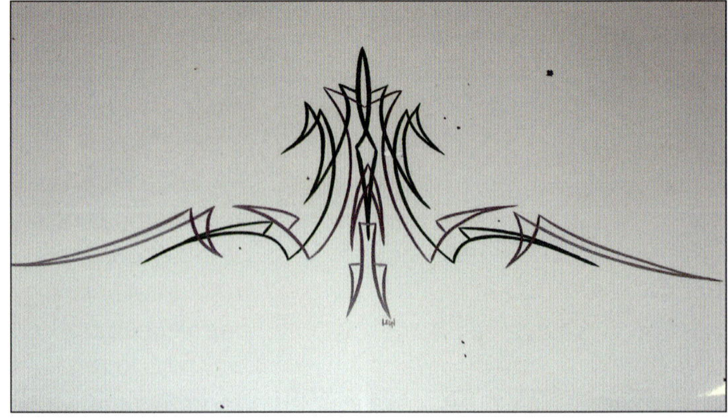

12 *After the paint has dried, lightly wipe some reducer over the panel to remove the Stabilo pen. The job is now complete.*

Ruben Castañon wanted one of these trucks for years. When he found this one almost abandoned in the desert, he had to have it. (Photo Courtesy Ruben Castañon)

Basic Bodywork

Bodywork is a complicated process that can be learned by anyone. However, it also takes a lot of time and experience to know what works best.

So, if you don't know how to do bodywork and you have the ability to pay for it, do that. It will be more than worth your money.

There are a few reasons to think about bodywork in this way. First, a completed paint job (or wrap) needs to go through a very specific sequence to come out correctly. The sequence includes metalwork, bodywork, primer, blocking, another round of priming and blocking, and paint. Each step builds on top of the other. By the time it's done, the goal is to have a perfectly flat panel that doesn't detract from the look of the truck.

How does one get that perfectly flat panel? Feel. A lot of professional body men use their hand and sense of touch to dial in where there are waves and where there aren't waves. The primer and guide coat are also your friend, as they'll show the low spots.

This process takes time to learn and learn well. You may not have the ability or the time necessary for your truck, or you may have such complex needs that things are just above your skill level. Don't feel bad about it. Just be prepared to pay appropriately for whatever you need.

In addition, set your expectations properly. For a black truck that's laser straight, doing the bodywork takes more than a good weekend with a sanding block. That means weeks and sometimes months of work that takes into consideration things such as shrink back. Patience is key.

Paint Job Walkthrough

Let's put all of this into practice. In this case, we have Ruben Castañon's Chevy Tahoe. This non-running truck was found in Southern Arizona and was purchased a few years ago for $1,000. That's a criminally low price for that truck, even though it wasn't in awesome shape. He was very excited about the deal.

Castañon had a plan. He wanted to build the exact truck that he would have owned back in the late 1990s if he been able to afford it. That meant he was going to paint the truck a factory color (Victory Red) and add a few other details here and there. He wasn't going to slam it, and he didn't need huge wheels. This was going to be period correct but still a head turner.

The interior was in bad shape. The stock leather was trashed, and the rest of the truck didn't look much better. (Photo Courtesy Ruben Castañon)

Beginning the Teardown

1 *First, Castañon assessed the damage. In this case, he is looking at the dent in the fender. He determined which parts he needed to replace and then made a budget. (Photo Courtesy Ruben Castañon)*

2 *Most of the interior was in pretty bad shape, so Castañon stripped out everything. Then, he cleaned the truck with a heavy degreaser. (Photo Courtesy Ruben Castañon)*

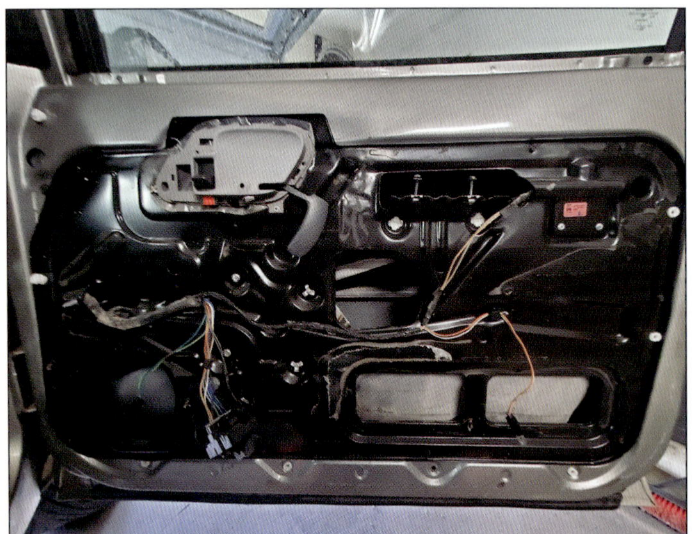

3 *The door panels were in pretty bad shape, so the only parts that he left were the power window and handle panel, and that wasn't even functional on the driver's side. (Photo Courtesy Ruben Castañon)*

4 *The engine bay was cleaned, and any loose ends were removed. Of course, there is no motor in this photo, but that was taken care of later. (Photo Courtesy Ruben Castañon)*

Bodywork Begins

1 The body shop performed its assessment and marked issues and what would be removed. Note the "shave" note by the antenna. (Photo Courtesy Ruben Castañon)

2 This was the first pass with the bodywork. Not everything was complete at this point, but notice how some areas are feathered out. That's what straight bodywork looks like. (Photo Courtesy Ruben Castañon)

3 Next, it was time for an initial prime. This would allow the shop to wet sand the entire truck to ensure that everything was straight. (Photo Courtesy Ruben Castañon)

4 The rear of the Tahoe received the same treatment. Note that the roll pan has also been welded on and bodyworked. (Photo Courtesy Ruben Castañon)

Paint and Reassembly

1 The truck was painted Victory Red. It looks straight, and even though it needs to be reassembled, the bones of what it will be are visible. (Photo Courtesy Ruben Castañon)

2 Next, the doors, fenders, and hood were sprayed. (Photo Courtesy Ruben Castañon)

3 The Tahoe's body didn't have much rust, but the underside wasn't great. Castañon wanted to go the extra mile though, so he separated the chassis from the cab so that he could get the bottom sprayed. (Photo Courtesy Ruben Castañon)

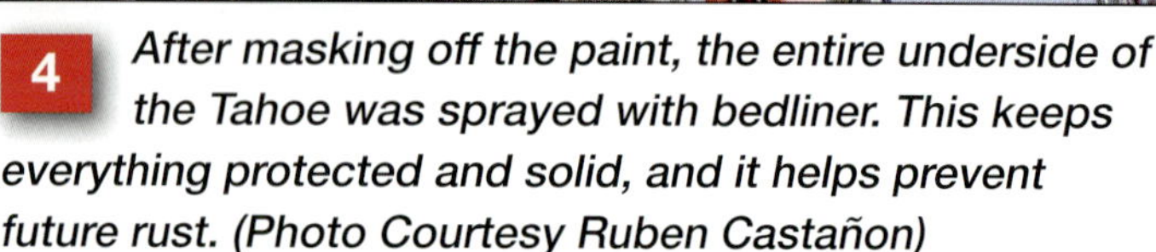

4 After masking off the paint, the entire underside of the Tahoe was sprayed with bedliner. This keeps everything protected and solid, and it helps prevent future rust. (Photo Courtesy Ruben Castañon)

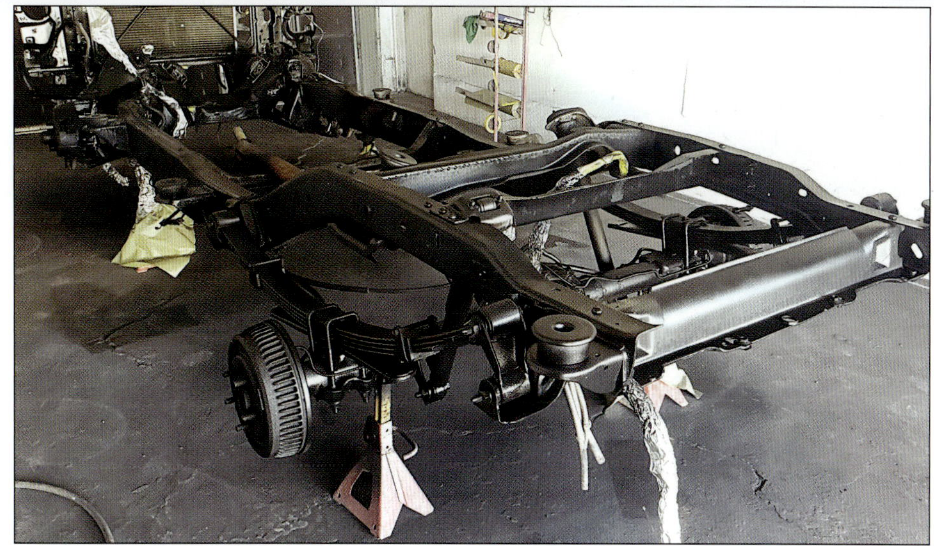

5 *Since it was all disassembled anyway, the body shop sprayed the entire frame black as well. Castañon didn't have the rest of the frame powder coated because he still had work to do on the chassis, but this was done to provide some protection. (Photo Courtesy Ruben Castañon)*

6 *Everything has been painted and was reassembled onto the truck, giving Castañon a great place to start on everything else. (Photo Courtesy Ruben Castañon)*

7 *This is the completed truck. (Photo Courtesy Ruben Castañon)*

CHAPTER 9

INTERIOR

The interior of a truck is where an owner spends the majority of his or her time, particularly if the truck is driven regularly. That's why it's one of the more fun areas to modify. After all, you should be comfortable when sitting behind the wheel, and the interior should look good.

In the 1990s, many aftermarket accessories were offered for these trucks, particularly for the interior. After much of that market segment had died down, companies rose up to breathe new life into it.

Disassembly

Everything begins with taking apart the truck. To do so, some tools are required. Many parts in these trucks are attached to the sheet metal with clips. These plastic tabs push into holes, and separating the two components can be a pain. The solution is to use trim panel removal tools. These are usually made of plastic, so they don't scratch anything, but metal versions are available as well. They have various shapes and are designed to fit behind whatever panels are necessary.

As mentioned in chapter 3, disassembling a truck requires you to be organized, and this is particularly true with the interior. With all of the various parts of the project, such as bodywork, paint, and chassis work, you may remove the interior and not reinstall it for more than a year. So,

The two red-and-black-handled tools are metal-clip removal tools. The shiny metal one in the top right is for removing the clips behind window-crank handles.

This kit features plastic tools. Each one is positioned or angled to remove a specific type of clip without scratching the surrounding surfaces. This kit is handy and affordable.

pay attention to what goes where so that parts don't get lost.

The other key point is to be careful during the disassembly itself. Even with a 1998 truck, the interior plastics are at least 26 years old. So, they may have dry rotted and are, at the bare minimum, fragile. Most of these trucks weren't garage kept with low mileage; they were instead driven hard and kept outside. The dashboards in particular get hit really hard, so handle them with care and store components so that there isn't too much weight on them.

Dashboards

If you can find an OBS truck with a dashboard that's in good shape, buy it. It doesn't matter if the truck is a piece of garbage or not, because that dashboard is worth its weight in gold.

This is particularly true of the 1995–1998 models, but the same thing applies to every year of OBS. The dashboard has a couple of key mounts. There are two down low that hold a steel cage to the firewall, and there are a few up top that hold the plastic to the body near the windshield. There is no reinforcement behind these panels.

This stress crack (and all of them that are shown) is on a 1998 Centurion. It's near the bezel and just above the gauges, which is where the dash tends to crack.

The other crack isn't lonely because there's yet another one just above the stereo.

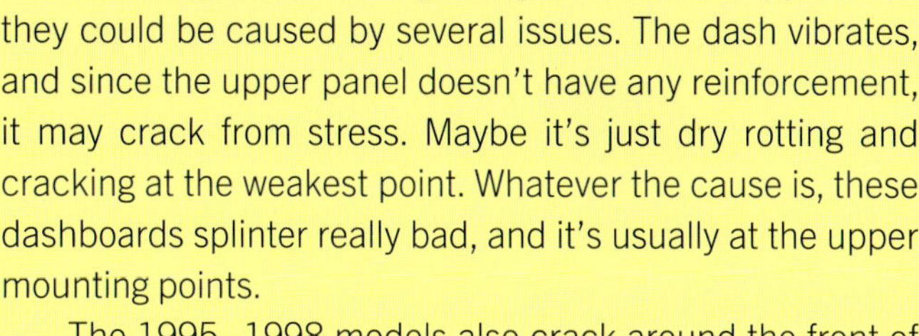

I can only speculate regarding how cracks happen, and they could be caused by several issues. The dash vibrates, and since the upper panel doesn't have any reinforcement, it may crack from stress. Maybe it's just dry rotting and cracking at the weakest point. Whatever the cause is, these dashboards splinter really bad, and it's usually at the upper mounting points.

The 1995–1998 models also crack around the front of the dash. If the truck has an aftermarket stereo and the goal is to take off the bezel, be careful. Even when it was new, the bezel was placed by slightly flexing the dash. This can also cause cracks. Some trucks have literally no top half to their dashboard for this very reason.

So, take care of the dash if it's in good shape. If it's in bad shape, find a replacement and take care of it. Maybe get a spare dash and hang on to it (just in case). ■

This spot has a crack that bridges the defroster vents (a notorious weak point), and it has been ovalled out too.

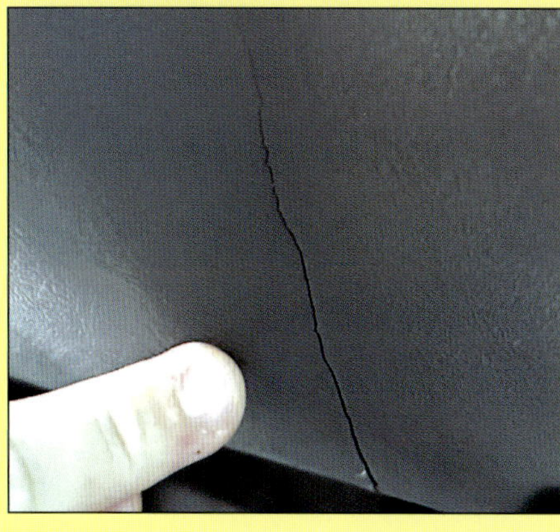

Not to be left behind, this is the knee panel just below the steering wheel. This isn't quite as common of a spot to crack.

Wrapping Panels

To modify the interior of your truck, one option is to upholster the plastic surfaces. In the 1990s, tweed was the material of choice, and everything was wrapped in a variation on the material. Today, suede and leather are common options.

Weldwood is sold in a spray can such as this, but it costs more per ounce than it does in a 5-gallon bucket. The bucket is cheaper, but you need to spray it using a suction-feed high-volume, low-pressure (HVLP) gun.

This is one of those tasks that can be done by an amateur, but it requires practice. The headliner is an easy enough place to start. With that being said, the type of adhesive that is used for the job is important.

Securing fabric to a vinyl or plastic panel requires a contact adhesive. This means that both surfaces are sprayed with a thin coat of the material. Then, once the adhesive is tacky, the two surfaces can be placed on top of each other, creating a bond.

The brand of contact adhesive that is used is critical. Look for Weldwood Contact Adhesive, and not 3M Super 88. When Weldwood Contact Adhesive is applied properly it locks the two components together and will do so for years. The Super 88 adhesive will eventually sag and give out in hot environments. Those in the southern United States can expect to get no more than a year out of that glue.

However, Super 88 might work well for you. Just know that the professionals use Weldwood.

Bucket Seat Swaps

OBS trucks had various seating options, depending on the year. The first option was a simple bench seat, which was commonly found on the lower-end models, such as the Cheyenne. Then, there was the 60/40 split bench, which was common and was in all sorts of models. Finally, there were bucket seats with a center console. These could be found in Suburbans

Painting the Interior

Another option for the interior is to paint everything. There are limits, but if you want to take the plastic or vinyl parts and lay down a color and/or graphics, you're in good company.

While this is a time-consuming option, it can look great when it's done. Just follow the same procedures as any paint job. ■

The owner of this truck didn't upholster his interior. Instead, he painted all of the plastic surfaces.

The graphics on the outside of the truck extend to the interior on the door panels.

and SUVs, but they weren't as common on trucks.

If the truck came with a bench seat, moving to a split bench or buckets requires drilling some holes. The same applies to split-bench offerings, as they still needed holes for the console and the inside rail of the seat.

Fortunately, swapping these seats isn't difficult or time consuming to do. In this case, the truck was already equipped with a stock-floor body drop, so the console needed some specific attention. Otherwise, it was a fairly straightforward installation.

Removing the Factory Seats

1 *This truck came with a 60/40 split bench. The center console pivots to become a seat back, but they're notorious for breaking.*

2 *Use a 15-mm socket to remove the bolts that attach the factory seats. Pull out the seats carefully. They're heavy, so consider asking a buddy for help.*

3 *After removing the seats, the problem is clear: it's missing some holes.*

Mounting the New Seats

1 *The new seat is electric, which is a nice bonus. Bolting it in place starts by securing it. In this case, the bolts are installed near the doorjamb.*

2 *Mark where the carpet needs some work. Use a paint marker to show where the holes need to go.*

Mounting the New Seats *continued*

3 *Even though not all of the carpet will be removed, marking where the seat sits can help to visualize the limits. If the carpet is cut outside of the line, it will be visible.*

4 *With the seat back out, cut a hole in the carpet with a razor blade.*

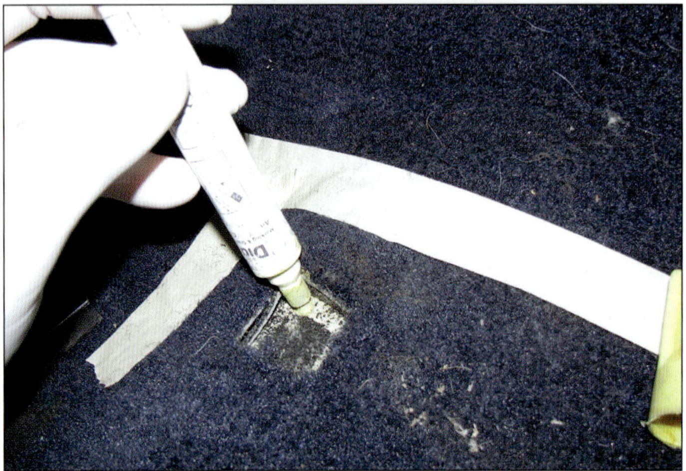

5 *Mark the carpet hole onto the sound deadener using the same paint marker. Remove the sound deadener in this area.*

6 *Removing the Dynamat requires cutting the material with a razor blade and then using a heat gun to loosen it up. It's important to clean it entirely. Otherwise, the drill bit could be ruined.*

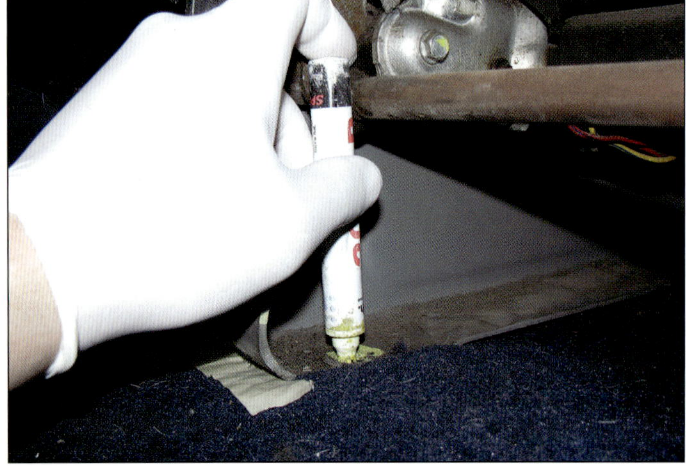

7 *Next, reinstall the seat to make marks for the actual bolt holes.*

8 *Drill the holes. Use progressively larger bits until the hole is the correct size.*

9 With the seat in place, bolt it to the chassis. It is possible to weld the mounting bolts to the cab, but washers and lock washers do the job just as well.

Mounting the Center Console

1 Place the center console into the cab. The center pocket is removable, which provides complete access to the mounting bolts.

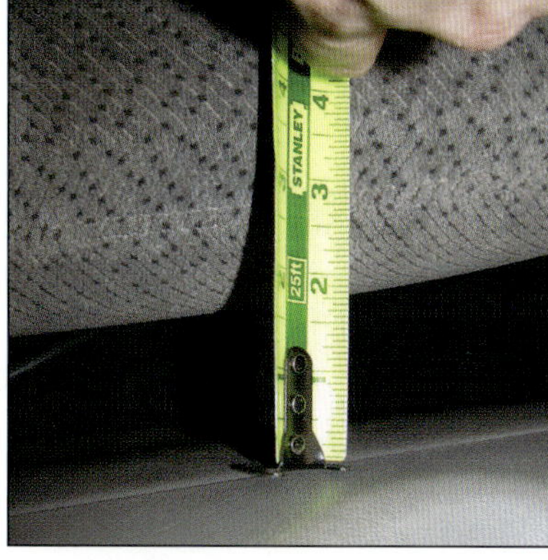

2 Although it seems obvious, measure to ensure that the console is centered between the two buckets.

3 This particular truck had the transmission tunnel modified, so the center console needed to lift up just slightly to clear. One-inch square tubing was used as a spacer to make up the difference. Since it needed to go against the floor, the carpet was marked with the paint marker.

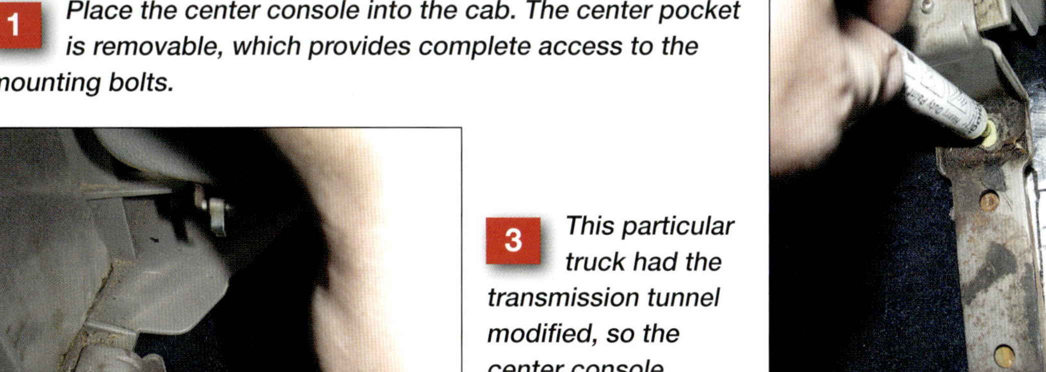

4 The paint marker shows where the holes are needed.

5 The resulting spacer with mounts was drilled out properly so that it would sit under the console.

Mounting the Center Console *continued*

6 *After painting the spacer, bolt down the console using the new hardware.*

7 *The completed setup is ready to go. Now, the truck just needs matching seat belts and/or new upholstery.*

Reupholstering Seats

Chances are good that the stock seat or seats in your truck are trashed or dirty. These are trucks after all, so finding a cigarette burn or just general grime in the fabric isn't shocking. If you're lucky enough to have factory leather, it's probably cracked and damaged.

The solution is to reupholster the seat(s). The cost of doing so varies widely, and it's based on the material that is used and how many seats will be reupholstered. Expect to pay $1,000 on the low end or more likely $2,000 for the job. Add new foam and maybe even new springs, depending on the shape of the original seat(s). If you want real leather, consider doubling the cost.

Steering Wheels

These trucks are unique in that they're the first Chevy bodystyle to integrate a driver-side and then a passenger-side airbag. Depending on the year of your OBS truck, it may have just one or both of these safety features, which have been proven to save lives.

Your opinion on whether or not you want an airbag in your truck is your own. Removing an airbag in a vehicle that's on the road is not allowed by the National Highway Traffic Safety Administration (NHTSA). Even getting an "On/Off Switch" requires NHTSA authorization, which is a lot of work to go through just to have a shiny steering wheel.

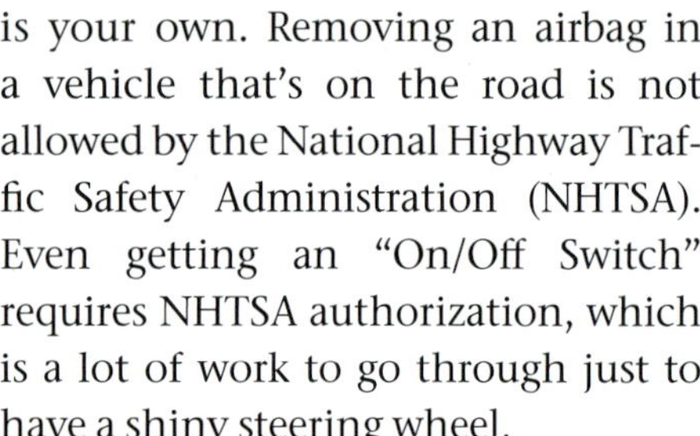

If the vehicle will be registered as a show truck or if it will only be trailered to events, you're free to do whatever you want. It won't see the road, so it doesn't matter. Just know that removing airbags is not the safe option.

Of course, if you have a 1988–1993 truck, there were no airbags, so do what you want. In addition, some cool steering wheel options are available.

Everything begins with a way to adapt the steering column's splined end with the steering wheel. Naturally, that part is called an adapter. Adapters range in price, depending on what you want. For example, a billet steering wheel adapter for these trucks is roughly $70 from the manufacturer. Sometimes a company will sell the adapter and steering wheel as one piece, but generally they're two separate components.

These seats were upholstered in leather and suede, but many options are available. It is possible to change patterns, colors, or textures to create whatever you want.

So, what kind of steering wheel should you get? Arguably the most popular type is a billet steering wheel. These are usually made of one chunk of aluminum (just like the rims), and they have a half-leather wrap so that you don't burn yourself in the summer. They come in a variety of diameters—from about 13.5 to 15 inches.

If going the pro-touring or pro-street route, there are other options as well. Sparc Industries sells some steering wheels that have a "factory custom" look. They're not cheap, though. The Muscle series starts at $1,195, and that's without the leather wrap. However, they're good looking, and they could be the perfect accent piece for your truck.

Installing a Billet Steering Wheel

The process of installing a billet steering wheel isn't difficult. It can be done in less than an hour and with only a few special tools. When working with an airbag-equipped truck, make sure to disconnect the battery first. Otherwise, you risk serious injury.

Prepping the Installation

1 *For an airbag-equipped truck, the first step is to disconnect the battery. Otherwise, if anything goes wrong, there is a risk of popping the airbag and potentially causing serious harm in the process.*

2 *With the truck parked and the emergency brake applied, the truck is locked with the steering wheel centered and the tires in the forward position.*

3 *Pull the tilt steering column lever out of the column by pulling it straight.*

4 *A pair of T-25 Torx-head bolts are located under the steering column. Unbolt them with the appropriate socket or bit and set them aside.*

Prepping the Installation *continued*

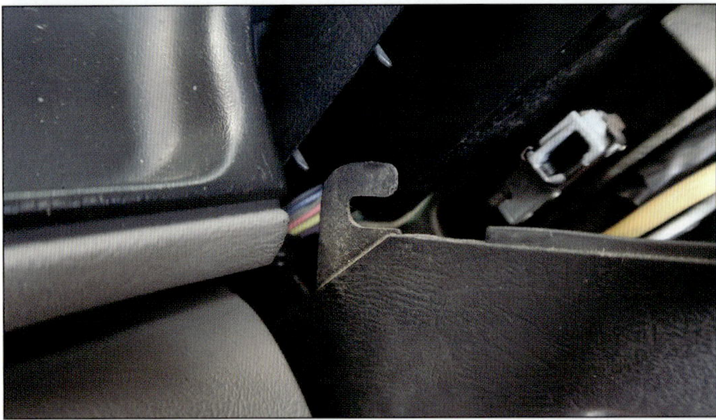

5 *The lower part of the column hinges on the top part. Pull it down by the steering wheel and then unhook it on the back.*

Removing the Steering Wheel

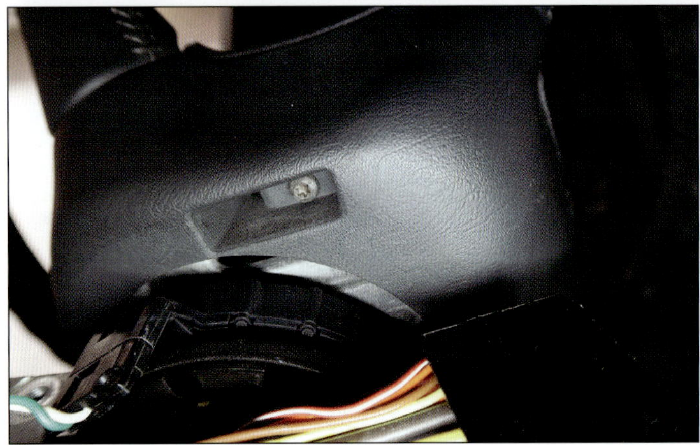

1 *Unlock the steering wheel and turn it 90 degrees in either direction. Look on the backside to find a T-20 Torx-head bolt. Remove it and then turn the steering wheel 180 degrees. Repeat this process on the other side.*

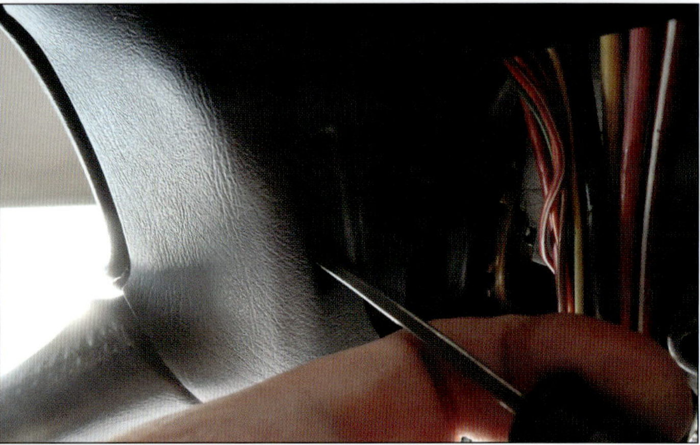

2 *Spring clips are in the same pockets as the Torx-head bolts. Use a flathead screwdriver to apply pressure and pop the airbag loose. Use the screwdriver like a lever, pulling away from the steering wheel.*

3 *Turn the airbag over and remove the black retainer. Then, pull the airbag harness out of the back of the airbag.*

4 *Return the steering wheel to center and lock it in place. Look closely for an alignment arrow by the steering-wheel nut. That's the top center.*

Removing the Steering Wheel *continued*

5 *Unbolt the 21-mm nut in the center of the steering wheel and set it aside.*

6 *Bolt a steering-wheel puller onto the steering wheel. Tighten down the center bolt until the wheel pops free.*

Removing the Clock Spring

1 *Next, remove the clock spring. This contains the wiring for the airbag, so it's unnecessary. Use a 4-mm socket to loosen the bolts that hold the top of the column cover in place.*

2 *Use a pair of snap-ring pliers to remove the snap ring that holds the clock spring to the column. Then, remove the clock spring by gently pulling the plastic off the clips. Disconnect it at the other end of the harness too, as it's right underneath the center of the dashboard.*

Installing the New Wheel

1 *First, install the billet steering-wheel adapter. Line it up so that the top hole is centered and the large hole on the inside for the horn button is over the column for the horn button.*

2 *Tighten the 21-mm steering-column bolt onto the column to secure the adapter into place.*

3 *Place the horn-button wiring that was provided with the kit into the horn-button hole on the adapter.*

4 *Secure the steering wheel to the adapter with a 3/32 Allen wrench or bit.*

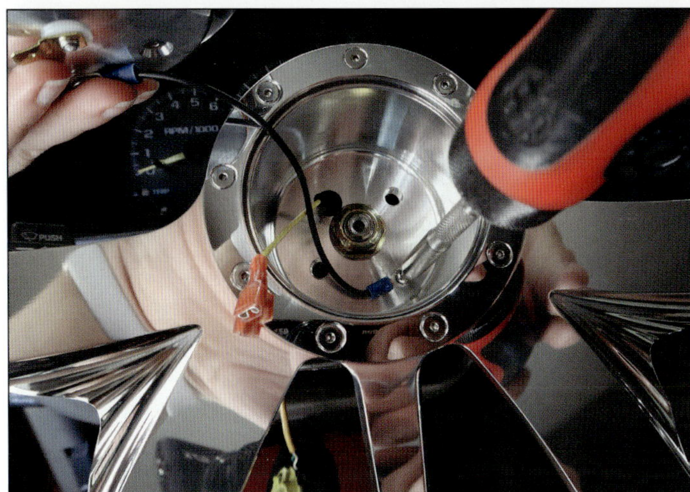

5 *With the help of an assistant, secure the black wire onto the back of the horn button to the inside of the adapter. Then, clip the spade terminal on the horn-button wiring to the backside of the button.*

6 *Lubricate the O-ring on the backside of the horn button. Then, push it into the adapter.*

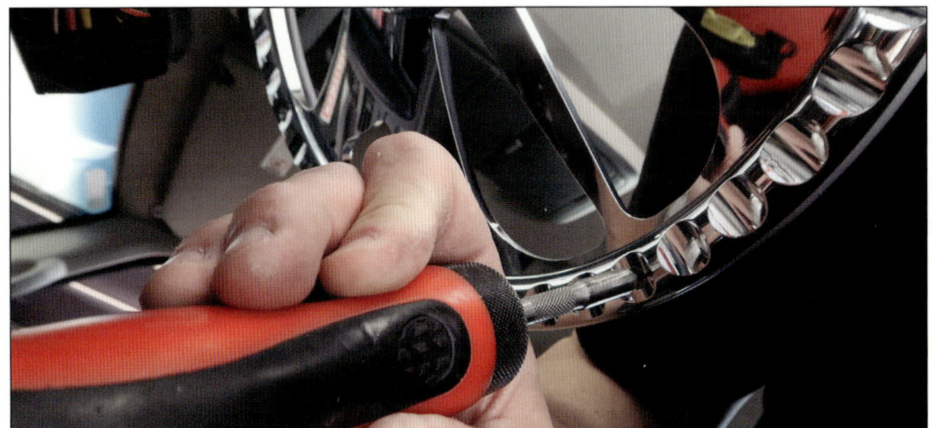

7 *Use the same 3/32 bit or Allen wrench to install the leather steering-wheel ring to the wheel. These mount from the backside, but once you get them lined up, it is smooth sailing.*

8 *Reinstall the column covers, and the installation is done. The steering wheel is complete.*

LG Billet

If your aim is to build a period-correct OBS truck, it must have billet accessories. When these trucks were produced, aftermarket companies sold several types of billet parts—from window cranks to stepside plates. Then, somewhere along the way, the well dried up. Sure, some billet parts were available, but they either didn't fit right or looked horrible. Fans had to turn to eBay and Facebook Marketplace to find what they needed secondhand. It was kind of a mess.

Then came LG Billet. The company began popping up in Instagram feeds with a billet shifter, then it made billet climate control knobs, and the parts list kept growing. It seemed like the company had a new OBS part every week, and then it expanded to NBS and beyond. It was pretty exciting.

What makes the company so special? It's not just that it's making a product people have demanded for years now. Its billet parts have a specific feel to them. They look industrial but clean. The pieces aren't polished, but they don't need to be because the machine work is perfect. Since the company has so many options available, you can fully billet-ize your truck and still get excited for what comes next. LG Billet even has interior door handles now.

So, if you're looking for billet parts for your OBS truck, this is your one-stop shop. ■

This is just one of the CNC machines that is used at LG Billet's facilities in Chandler, Arizona. (Photo Courtesy LG Billet)

These OBS climate-control knobs are fresh out of the CNC machine. (Photo Courtesy LG Billet)

These OBS climate-control knobs are ready for packaging. (Photo Courtesy LG Billet)

Billet Accessories

In the 1990s, it was difficult to find one of these trucks without billet accessories, including dash kits, door sills, column shifters, etc. If it was able to be unbolted or was a flat enough surface to be stuck to, you could find billet parts for it.

Today, those parts are getting difficult (but not impossible) to find. Billet and Acrylic Fantasies was one of the bigger shops when these trucks were produced, and it now sells its wares on eBay. A company named Maxxtech.com purchased a good portion of billet accessories from Empire Motorsports, and it's been selling what it has left. Now, the company is based in Germany, so parts delivery is not quick. However, the parts are straight out of the 1990s, which is tough to beat.

Of course, other materials are popular today, including carbon fiber and wood. However, if you want accessories that provide a true feel from the era when these trucks were produced, billet is the best option.

Installing Billet Door Sill Plates

Billet door sill plates can be installed over the existing units or can be a direct replacement, depending on what kind you get.

1 *These sill plates are from Empire Motorsports, so they're difficult to find today. Fortunately, there are alternatives.*

2 *Remove or loosen the seat-belt bolt. It has a T-50 Torx head.*

3 *These particular plates go over the existing models, so they're easy to install. Just unscrew the originals.*

4 *Slide in the new ones. Then, screw them into place. It's that simple.*

5 *After the seat-belt retractor has been bolted back into place, the job is complete.*

Installing a Billet Grab Handle

The stock A-pillar on a truck usually has a grab handle on the passenger's side to make getting into the truck easier when it's at the stock height. There's no reason not to replace it with something better, such as this one from LG Billet.

1 *The stock handle has two plastic covers that hide the stock bolts. Remove it with a ratchet and socket. After the two bolts have been removed, pull the handle off the pillar.*

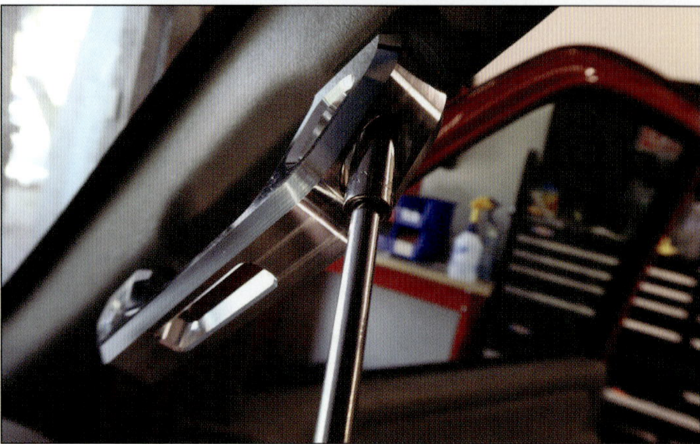

2 *Now, the new handle can be installed with the stock bolts.*

3 *The completed handle looks significantly better.*

Installing a Billet Automatic Shifter Handle

Two types of shifter handles are available for these trucks, depending on the year. The 1988–1994 trucks use a different one than the 1995–1998 trucks, so purchase the correct one.

1 *The billet shifter looks much better than the stock shifter. It's a much cleaner look overall.*

Installing a Billet Automatic Shifter Handle *continued*

2 Remove the stock shifter with a Torx-head socket.

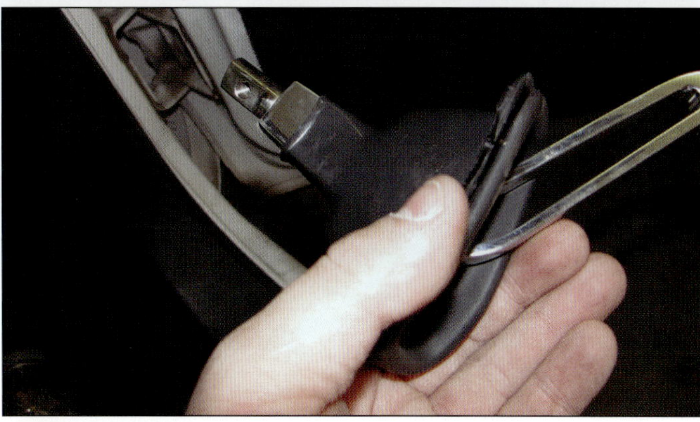

3 The existing shifter boot was ripped, so install a new one. It just slid in place over the shifter before installation to make life easier.

4 Now, slide the shifter into the existing mount and reinstall the bolt.

5 Meanwhile, the boot slides into the steering-column cover with no problems.

Installing a Billet Rearview Mirror

A simple and easy accessory for a truck's interior is the rearview mirror. It's not extremely expensive (Billet Specialties sells one for $90), and it takes less than 5 minutes to install.

1 Here's the new billet rearview mirror. The slot in the mount is where it will sit on the window.

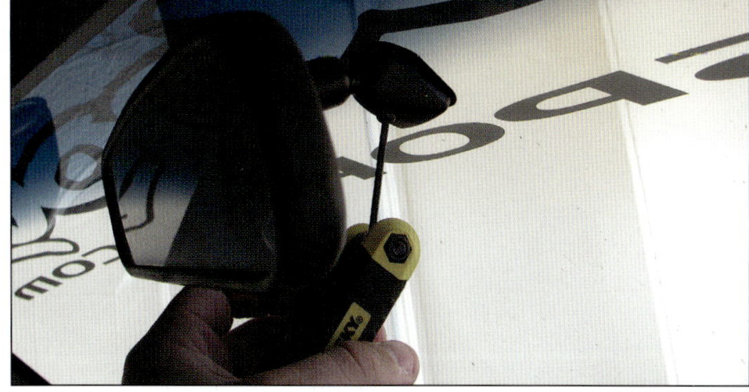

2 The factory rearview mirror is attached to the windshield mount with a Torx-head screw. Remove the screw, and the mirror will slide up and off the windshield.

Installing a Billet Rearview Mirror *continued*

3 *This is the result. If this mount isn't on your truck, don't worry; AutoZone and other parts stores stock it. You can put a new one on with the appropriate adhesive. Then, slide the replacement mirror on and tighten the screw.*

Installing Billet Pedals

Installing billet pedals is one of the easiest things to do, and it's something that's often overlooked. Brightening up the pedals with billet or deciding to do something more understated can give the inside of a truck a more high-end look than the utilitarian feel that the stock pedals and rubber covers provide. In addition, they're affordable. Billet Specialties sells a universal set for $140.

1 *The stock accelerator pedal has a clip on the side that holds it in place. Remove the clip with a flathead screwdriver and slide the pedal off of the linkage. Don't forget to slide off the spring too.*

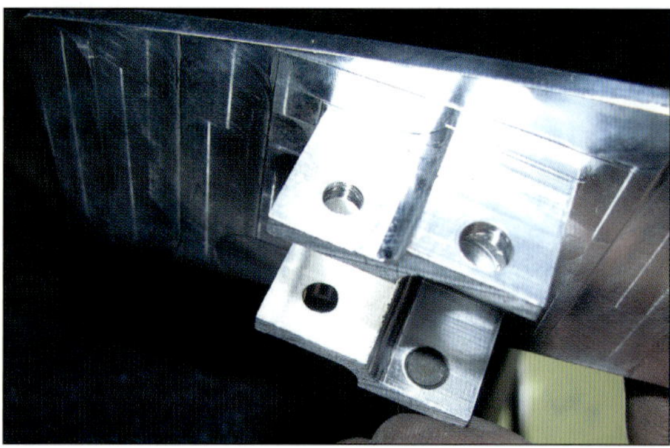

2 *There are two different mounting points on the pedal, which provides options. The idea is the same as the stocker pedal. Slide the linkage through the first hole, put on the spring, and then slide the linkage through the second hole.*

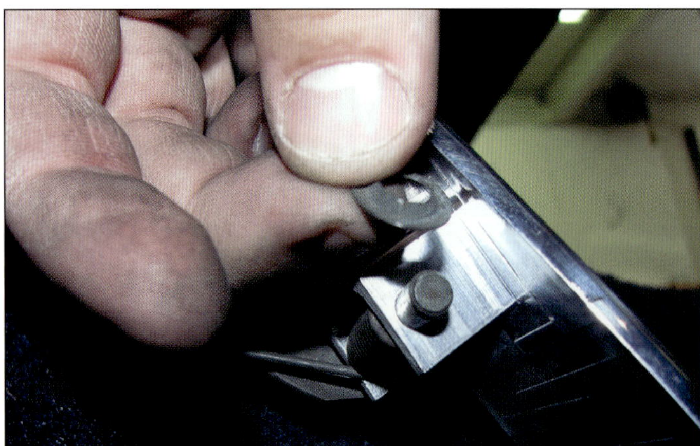

3 *With the spring and linkage installed, the only thing that remains is to reinstall the factory washer.*

4 *To remove the brake pedal, remove the cover by peeling it off the pedal.*

Installing Billet Pedals *continued*

5 *Mark the centerline of the pedal, and then use the template that came with the kit to mark the corners for drilling.*

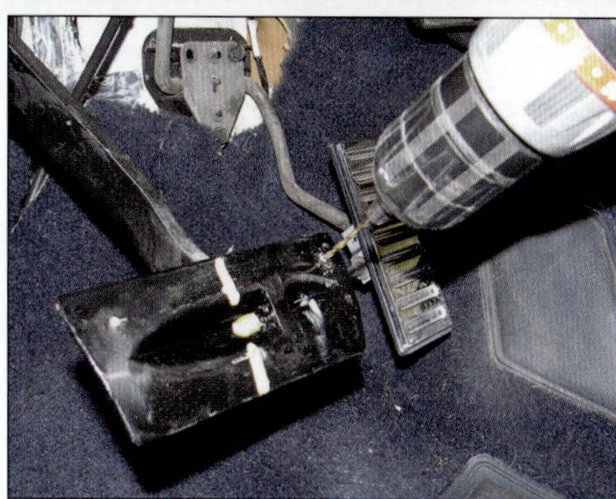

6 *Drill each hole with successively larger bits until it comes to the final size.*

7 *Finally, tighten the bolts in place, securing the new billet pedal to the stock one.*

Installing a Billet Gauge Cluster Surround

The stock gauge cluster is nice and functional. If you're not planning to replace it entirely with something digital (which is certainly an excellent idea), the next-best thing is to dress it up by installing a billet gauge cluster surround. These slim pieces of metal fit around the cluster, which provides something shiny around the gauges.

1 *Pull the dash bezel off the front of the dash. It pulls off with a firm tug, but an automatic shifter does get in the way. You can always shift the truck into low gear if it's parked and chocked.*

2 *Four bolts hold the cluster in place. Unbolt them and slide it out as an assembly.*

Installing a Billet Gauge Cluster Surround *continued*

3 *Here is the basic layout of how the two pieces will line up. Empire Motorsports no longer makes these, but they can be found on eBay and the like.*

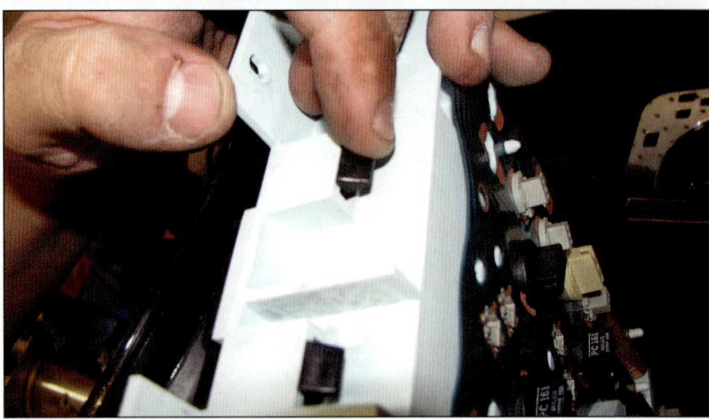

4 *Four clips hold the Plexiglas cover to the cluster. Depress them until they pop free.*

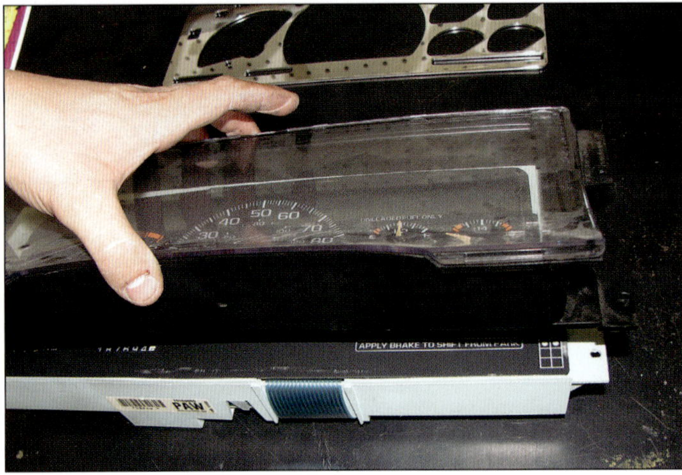

5 *Carefully lift the cover off and place it to the side. It's important not to get dust in the system.*

6 *There are adhesive circles placed strategically around the billet piece. Once the gauges are clean, set them into place.*

7 *Line up the bezel and carefully stick it down to the cluster. Wipe off any fingerprints with a microfiber towel and do the same with the inside of the plastic cover. Reassemble, and it is good to go.*

Installing a Billet Headlight Switch and Climate Control Bezels

There are two spots on the interior that look really good with billet accessories, but don't overdo it. Those items are the climate controls and the headlight bezel. They can be found on eBay (Billet and Acrylic sells them there), as well as other spots online, but the basic idea is to brighten up the inside a bit without going overboard.

1 *The headlight bezel sticks to the stock headlight switch just like the gauge cluster. However, in this case, don't remove the switch. If you did, you risk having some of the billet under the dash bezel.*

2 *After peeling off the adhesive, stick down the bezel.*

3 *The process for the climate-control bezel is the same. The only thing is to make sure to get the right one. The SUVs have an additional button, so that bezel is different than the bezel for the pickups.*

4 *Billet switches also are available for the climate controls. Pulling the originals off is usually pretty easy, but pliers are sometimes needed.*

5 *These switches are a two-piece design. First, install the base onto the original shaft and tighten it in place with the provided Allen-head set screw.*

6 *Attach the actual switch in the same fashion. This way, you can adjust where the pointer is aimed.*

7 *The completed panel is clean and simple. It just needs a quick polish.*

Installing a Billet Glove-Box Button

LG Billet makes a billet glove-box button with a stylized American flag etched into the material. It looks pretty sweet.

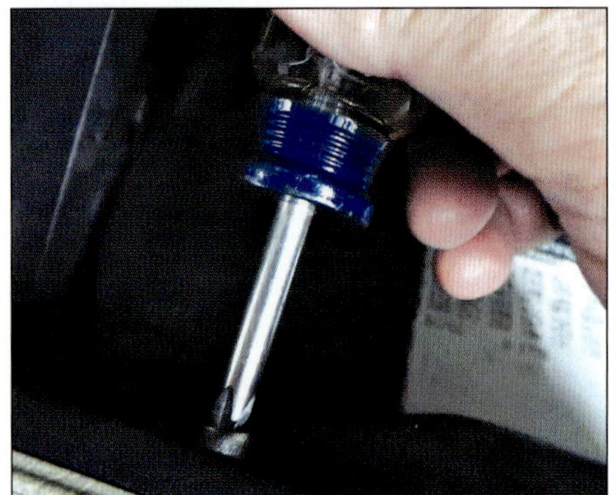

1 *Use a Philips-head screwdriver to remove the two screws that hold the stock button in place.*

2 *Remove the stock button. Twist it around to separate it from the linkage.*

3 *Then, slide the new button around the linkage in the reverse order.*

4 *The outer portion of the billet button (the part with the flag) slides over the button. Then, rotate the entire thing 180 degrees and hold it in place.*

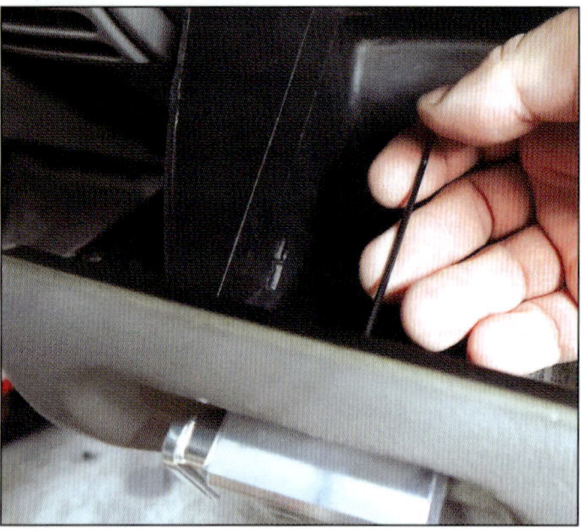

5 *Secure it in place with the provided Allen-head bolts.*

6 *The new handle adds a nice touch to the dash.*

Installing a Billet Column Tilt Lever

1 *This is probably the easiest billet part to install. First, pull the stock tilt-column adjuster out with your hand.*

2 *Then, install the new one. That's it!*

Wheels and Tires

The right set of wheels (also called rims) can make or break a truck. If you buy an inexpensive wheel, the finish may flake or the wheel could bend easily. If you select the wrong size, it might not work well with the appearance that you had in mind. There's a lot to consider.

With that in mind, I'll go over the various types of wheels that are available and what that will mean for your project.

Wheel and Tire Basics

Let's start with the basics. Whatever wheels are purchased need to fit certain criteria, particularly if they need to tuck inside the wheel wells or if the goal is for them to stick out. In addition, size is always a factor.

Size

I'll begin with the size of the wheels, specifically with the diameter. For OBS trucks, sizes start at 15 inches and go up to 26 inches (and higher). Your truck probably came with a 15-inch wheel from the factory, which is the minimum size that is required to fit the wheel over the brakes. Smaller wheels have interference issues.

Some people love using 15-inch wheels with big tires, while others want a 24-inch rim and the smallest sidewall that they can find. It's up to you which path you choose, but there are some things to consider before making a decision.

The biggest one is rotational mass. The heavier the wheels are, the more power it's going to take to turn them and to stop them. A set of 24-inch cast wheels will probably decrease the stopping distance a decent amount. Is that worth the trade-off?

There are ways to sort this out. Select a rim that's a compromise between the size wanted and the size that's better suited for the truck. Otherwise, upgrade the brakes to

The owner of this particular truck is a fan of staggered wheels. In this case, 22-inch billet wheels were installed in the back, and 20s were installed in the front.

compensate for the additional mass or order lighter wheels to get the size you want. It's part of the reason why you see people running large-diameter billet wheels: they're light and look cool.

Another factor is wheel width. While it could be cool to run a 20x11 on the front of your ride, there's no way to make that work without either heavily modifying the frame or having the wheels stick out past the stock fenders. The width that is chosen will determine how much of a dish will be on the rims and what offset you choose. While many things can be made to work, OBS owners normally use an 8.5- to 9-inch-wide wheel in the front, and a wheel from 8.5 to 10 inches in the back.

Backspacing and Offset

Other variables are wheel backspacing and offset. Imagine there's a wheel in front of you. Now, turn it to the side so that if the tire was on the rim, you'd be looking at the tread. If you were to measure from the wheel's face to the inside lip and split that distance in half, that point is known as the wheel's centerline. This is the basis for everything from here moving forward.

Note that the face of the wheel is the side where the lug nuts are screwed onto the studs to secure the wheel to the truck.

Backspacing is measured from the surface where the rim contacts the hub to the inside lip of the rim.

The wheel has a "zero" offset if the surface where the rim contacts the hub aligns with the centerline of the wheel. The wheel has a positive offset if the surface where the rim contacts the hub is closer to the face of the rim. The wheel has a negative offset if the surface where the rim contacts the hub is closer to the inside lip of the rim.

Why are these measurements important? There are a few reasons. As mentioned previously, having the wrong offset can cause issues with the brakes or other components hitting the rim. Sometimes that occurs when turning the wheel, and other times it occurs on the first mounting. It's why you don't usually see a wheel with a positive offset on a truck.

If you build a lowered truck, you

If you do a lot of wheel and tire fitment checks, buy a tool such as this one, which is pictured on a 1974 K5 Blazer. It's called the Wheel Tek Master Kit, and it's made by CCTek. (Photo Courtesy Switch Suspension)

Use this tool to properly determine the wheel offset that is needed to fit a particular tire. Since it's done on your vehicle, you'll know exactly what is needed before you spend the money. (Photo Courtesy Switch Suspension)

need to decide how low you want to go. If you're aiming to sit on the ground, then the rims need to tuck inside of the wheel wells and work with the tires. In addition, you need to consider turning the wheel while driving.

So, wheel offset is an important detail to look into before ordering your wheels. Figure out if the wheels will work for your project or measure yourself and use that information to get custom wheels built.

Finishes

A great thing about buying a set of wheels is that they can be customized even further to stand out. Ten of your friends may have the same design, but due to the variety in sizes, offsets, and finishes, your set can be unique.

The finish of the wheel is one of the first ways to attract attention. It is either the coating placed over the rim itself, or the way it's, well, finished. Dozens of options are available, and more are coming every day, so there's no way to create an exhaustive list of them all. However, since many of them use similar processes, the following content will provide a good idea of what to look for.

Polished finishes are popular. This style is used on many billet wheels, as they are made of aluminum, which is relatively easy to polish. It creates a mirror-like finish, but it will require maintenance unless it's covered with a clear powder coat. The maintenance includes using a microfiber towel and some aluminum polish when the finish gets dull. It's not a huge ordeal, but if you want to get the backside of the wheel as well, it involves putting the truck on jack stands.

Painting is another popular choice because it's accessible to almost everyone and pretty easy to do. Just like painting any other part, the surface must be prepped and everything that you don't want painted must be masked off. Some manufacturers offer painted wheels. It's not as durable as a powder coat, but it gets the job done.

Some manufacturers offer a variety of coatings for their wheels. Budnik, for example, offers titanium, charcoal, basalt, bronze, turbine, black, and silver ceramic. It can even do different finishes for the wheel center, outer rim, and center cap.

Powder coating is another option. It is a durable finish that can handle a lot of what the road throws at you. It's not perfect, as it can still chip. Many color options are available.

Many manufacturers (particularly of billet wheels) offer a brushed finish, which means that the grain of the wheel is visible and the wheel has a less-reflective shine. It's a cool thing to pair with another finish, such as polished or painted surfaces, or just to do on its own.

Chrome is a common finish. This is a plating process that provides a mirror-like finish on the wheel.

These wheels from the company US Mags have a black center, machined edges, and a polished lip. (Photo Courtesy Switch Suspension)

Because aluminum is so flexible, chrome-plated billet wheels aren't often found. However, chrome cast wheels are quite popular. They look good, and they're also easy to clean, requiring only glass cleaner and a microfiber towel. Chrome polish can be used, but it's not necessary every time they are cleaned.

It may seem like there are a lot of options to choose from because there are. But wait, there's more: you're not always restricted to just one finish. For example, Raceline offers billet wheels with a show polish and painted spokes. Of course, you can always do that on your own.

Take your time and figure out what works best for you and your needs before pulling the trigger on a finish. You'll be happier in the long run.

Billet Wheels

When making the decision about rims for an OBS truck, the topic of billet or forged wheels is sure to come up. The term "billet," refers to a chunk of metal, but in the world of wheels, it's usually aluminum. That billet of aluminum is carved down to a specific size using special machinery. Then, it's ready to go.

Today, billet wheels are made in a variety of ways. The typical option is a billet center (the design of the wheel) that's carved out of aluminum and then installed into a hoop to form a completed rim. In addition, there are three-piece wheels that are two pieces of a hoop and a center that all bolt together as well as wheels that are completely forged from one billet—wheel, hoop and all.

There are thousands of different ways that billet wheels are made, and the styles are seemingly infinite. The

Although these wheels are 20s and 22s, it's easy to see the offset difference between the front and rear wheels. That's one of the huge advantages of billet wheels. (Photo Courtesy Switch Suspension)

major advantage to most billet wheels is the ability to choose the offset.

Think about how the average wheel manufacturer works. It wants to produce one kind of wheel that has the best offset for that diameter in that bolt pattern for any number of vehicles. A stock, 2WD OBS truck has a 5x5 bolt pattern. The first number (5) is for the number of studs and the second number (5) is the bolt circle measurement. Note that the second number is an SAE measurement, but you might find wheels out there that are measured in metric. If so, you want a 5x127-mm bolt pattern.

Billet wheel manufacturers produce each wheel as they're ordered. So, if the goal is a 24x12 in the back and a 20x8 in the front, they can make that happen. In addition, you can even choose the finish, the bolt pattern, and the offset. It's up to you.

Billet wheels are much lighter than their cast counterparts. Lifting a 22-inch cast wheel with a tire mounted isn't a fun process, but doing it on a billet wheel is much easier. Aluminum is a strong, lightweight material. As a result, billet wheels have less rotational mass and it's not necessarily going to throw out your back to change a set of wheels.

Because of all of these things, billet wheels are not cheap. Don't be surprised to see them listed for $1,000 per rim. In addition, aluminum is strong, but it is also susceptible to bending. If you live in an area with horrible roads, get ready to fix your wheels a lot. They can bend if you're not careful, and it can get gnarly and expensive.

This is not meant to suggest shying away from billet wheels. Many of the big show trucks out there have billet wheels, and they're not bad to own if you're careful or have a large enough tire. Just know what you're getting into before spending your money.

Cast Wheels

On the other end of the spectrum are cast wheels. These are the mass-market rims that can be found at tire shops, such as Discount Tire, as well as online. They are available in many different finishes, and, depending on the brand, they can be pretty affordable too.

With billet or forged wheels, the rim is built via hunks of metal and a whole lot of machine work. Cast wheels also start with metal, but it's in liquid form. The manufacturer starts with a mold that's in the shape and design of the final product. The liquid aluminum is poured into the mold or a vacuum is used to draw it in. After it cools, the rim is complete—well, mostly. There's usually some trimming to do due to aluminum going into gaps in the mold. In addition, sometimes things need to be drilled out after the fact. However, for the most part, you have yourself a cast wheel.

Cast wheels have advantages and disadvantages. They're built, depending on the manufacturer, on a one-size-fits-all basis. For many years, that worked just fine for OBS owners because 5x5 was the dominant bolt pattern. However, today, more trucks use a six-lug configuration, so there aren't as many 5x5 options out there, and those that do sometimes don't fit the bill.

That's not to say that buying billet wheels is the only option—far from

This two-door Tahoe has 20-inch American Racing Novas, which are a cast wheel. They look great, they're affordable, and they still fit into the wheel wells. (Photo Courtesy Switch Suspension)

it. Just know that the options may be more limited with a cast wheel.

The cost is also a plus. Cast wheels cost significantly less than billet wheels, depending on the finish. Some people prefer chrome, and that isn't an option on a billet wheel, so cast is the only option. No matter what, a cast wheel will definitely cost less than its billet counterpart. For example, the American Racing Novas cost about $350/each.

The downside comes down to the casting process itself. While the aluminum (or other metal) is cooling, air bubbles can form. If the metal cools and those bubbles stay, they turn into voids that can either form rust (if it's not 100-percent aluminum) or lead to weakness and cracking. That means if you're driving on a cast wheel with a low-profile tire and hit a bump at the wrong spot, you could crack the rim.

A lot of this comes down to the quality of the cast wheel; some manufacturers have stricter casting processes than others. There are plenty of people out there rolling on cast wheels that have never had a crack or a flaw rear its ugly head. Just be aware of what's out there, and check with people about the brand's reputation. It's better to be safe than sorry.

How to Calculate Wheel and Tire Sizes

Up to this point, we've talked about rims. Now, it's time to get into the other part of the equation: tires. Without tires, rims are just going to look pretty while the truck is on jack stands.

Many different types of tires are available, but there are a few generalities that can be made. The lower the profile of the tire, the stiffer the ride will be. That's because there's very little give built into the sidewall. If there's not much give, it won't get any extra bounce. Second, the taller the tire, the smaller the rim will probably be—there's only so much room in a fender well.

You probably have a type of build in mind, and with it comes a general idea of the kind of tires you want. A pro-street build, for example, would have slicks on the rear, while a truck that's bagged may have the lowest-profile tires that are available. No matter if the build is for a lowered extra-cab or a body-dropped single cab, the height of the tires will be needed at some point. Otherwise, there will be interference issues and potentially problems driving.

Determining a tire size is an opaque process if you're just jumping into it. So, let's walk through the process.

Say that you want to buy 22-inch wheels for your truck, and you selected 265/35-22 tires. Perfect. This number will determine how much needs to be cut out of the inner fender wells, the size of the bridge, and the overall height compared to the stock tires.

That first number (265) is the width of the tire in millimeters. So, the hypothetical 265/35-22 is 265 mm wide. The second number is the percentage of the sidewall width that is the height of the tire, and it is referred to as the profile ratio (or aspect ratio). Let's turn this into an equation so it makes more sense.

X = Tire width (mm)
Y = Tire width (inches)
Z = Profile ratio
B = Sidewall height

Let's start by converting the width of the tire into inches to make life easier. The equation is pretty simple:

$$Y = X \div 25.4$$

That's because there's 25.4 mm per inch. Let's use the example tire size now:

$$Y = 265 \div 25.4$$
$$Y = 10.43 \text{ inches}$$

Now, let's plug this into the sidewall equation:

$$B = (Z \times Y) \div 100$$

Why divide by 100? It's because the number is a percentage. Now, plug in the numbers.

$$B = (35 \times 10.43) \div 100$$
$$B = (365.05) \div 100$$
$$B = 3.65 \text{ inches}$$

This provides the sidewall height. However, technically, that's only half. A tire goes all the way around a wheel, so technically we are looking for a top and a bottom. That means we want a different equation:

A = Overall tire height
C = Wheel diameter

$$A = (2B) + C$$
$$A = [2\,(3.65)] + 22$$
$$A = (7.3) + 22$$
$$A = 29.3 \text{ inches}$$

If you want to make things more fun (from a mathematical perspective), here's the whole thing in one formula:

$$[2\,(ZX \div 2540)] + C$$

Finally, we'll plug in our numbers again:

$$2\,[(265 \times 35) \div 2540] + 22$$
$$2\,(9{,}275 \div 2{,}540) + 22$$
$$2\,(3.65) + 22$$
$$7.3 + 22 = 29.3 \text{ inches}$$

Now, what does all this mean for the build?

To lower the truck so the frame sits on the ground, measure the distance between the bottom of the frame and the top of the bed and front fenders. That number will provide the maximum height wheel and tire that can fit under the sheet metal (assuming that wheel tubs are put in the back).

If you plan to body drop the truck, the same rule applies but with the bottom of the body.

There are some things to consider with that number. In the front, negative camber (the tendency for the top of the wheels to tilt inward toward the engine) causes that number to be a bit skewed, since the tire is now being measured on an angle and not flat. In addition, add in at least 1/2 inch of fudge room, as most tires expand when they heat up as you drive.

At the end of the day, knowing the wheel and tire size helps you select the optimal wheel and tire pairing for your vehicle.

What About the Speedometer?

In any kind of custom vehicle build where wheels and tires are a different diameter than stock, you may notice differences in how your speedometer is functioning. That's because when the overall wheel and tire diameter is larger than the stock set, the wheel has a larger circumference. That means it has fewer rotations than the stock setup had, which means the speedometer will read that the truck is going slower than it actually is. The odometer reading will be off as well. Going the opposite direction will cause the same thing in reverse.

The solution is to start with a baseline. A 1998 Chevrolet Silverado came with a 235/75-15 tire. That gives an overall diameter of 28.9 inches and a circumference of 90.7 inches.

If it is upgraded to a 22-inch wheel, the closest you could get is with a 255/35-22 tire. This would put it at a 29-inch diameter and 91-inch circumference. That's pretty close, and the speedometer would be fairly close to stock (albeit not perfect).

With a 24-inch wheel, the closest you can get is a 275/25-24. That has a 29.4-inch diameter and a 92.4-inch circumference. In this case, the speedometer would definitely be incorrect, and you would be traveling at a speed greater than what the dashboard shows.

Whether or not this is important to your build is up to you. However, it's important to note that changing the wheels and tires can affect the odometer, and that could affect the resale value of the truck (due to the odometer reading) later on.

15s to 26s

A 1988–1998 Chevy or GMC truck probably came with 15-inch wheels from the factory. That's fine for many people, but for a custom truck, you'll want to change out the rims and tires for something different. You can stick with 15-inch wheels if you like. They are the smallest size that can go on a truck safely without messing with the brakes. However, stockers don't fly on customs.

On the other end of the spectrum, some pretty big wheels can be installed on these trucks. There are plenty of guys that are body dropped on a 24-inch wheel and a super tiny tire. There are even videos of standard cabs rolling on 26s, if that's your thing. Options are available.

However, there are a few things that to consider. There is only so much room to work with under the sheet metal and with the suspension. That guy rolling on 26s? He's not very low. In addition, the body-dropped truck on 24s has a pretty stiff ride because those tires are rubber bands compared to the 15-inch stockers.

To go with a large-diameter rim and tire combination, think about not only the fender opening but also how much room you'll have to turn. How drivable is a truck with tires and wheels like that?

The choice is yours. Decide how drivable you want the truck to be, how comfortable it should be for you and your passengers, how low it can go, and what you're willing to give up to get some extra style points.

With that in mind, let's cover the basic options.

To go for an old-school look, or if you just prefer smaller wheels, consider anything from 15 to 18 inches. In the 1990s, when these trucks were new, 17s and 18s were all that anyone bought. Getting a set of 20s in 1999 was considered to be radical—the type of thing that only an extreme builder would or could do. Cutting the front coil pockets back then was a well-kept secret that was passed from builder to builder. They were good times.

Today, those smaller sizes are having a resurgence. People are springing up online selling "baby billets," which are billet aluminum wheels that are usually less than 18 inches in diameter. If your build is aiming for nostalgia or being period correct, consider going this route.

One could make the argument that the standard wheel size for these trucks is a 20. An OBS can lay frame on a 20 without too many crazy modifications, and they fill up the wheel well nicely. You can even put a decently sized tire on them at that size, providing a more comfortable ride. They're available, popular, and easy to find without having to get something custom made. These are also great for a truck with coilovers, as the truck can be set low enough to look good, and it will handle great as well.

These are the popular 454/Sport wheels from the early 1990s. They're pretty sharp for a stock 15-inch wheel. (Photo Courtesy Switch Suspension)

Bigger wheels means smaller tires. A 22-inch wheel is usually a decent compromise because you can put a relatively large tire on one and the truck is still drivable, even with a body drop. Most (but not all) people with 22s tend to be bagged. They're not really the best size for a coilover-equipped truck (at least not in the front), nor anything else that sits pretty low. If the truck has an adjustable suspension, they look great tucked up in the wheel wells.

Then, there's 24-inch wheels and those that are larger. As mentioned before, you can make them work on trucks that aren't bagged, but the ride will look like it's lifted. These wheels are so big that they give the truck the appearance that it's stock height or taller, even if it's not. That's not necessarily a bad thing, and it's definitely a style that some people want. Just remember the tradeoffs when putting together the project.

Big Wheels and Body Drops

For the purposes of this discussion, let's define a "big wheel" as anything over 20 inches in diameter. Although no one would really consider a 20 to be mammoth, it's a good starting point.

When body dropping a truck with a larger wheel, consider the overall diameter of the wheel, the depth of the tire and wheel combination, and how much clearance is needed to turn. Let's tackle these point by point.

The diameter of the wheel affects how much is cut out of the firewall and the fenders. The fenders are relatively easy to deal with, as it just involves unbolting the stock liner and then coming up with new mounts for the various accessories. However, the firewall will require cutting and then building a new tub. The wiring harness will also have to be repositioned, as it'll be in the way.

The larger the wheel, the bigger the fender cutouts and firewall tubs will be—that much is obvious. However, at some point, particularly with a body drop, it's going to encroach on the legs in the passenger compartment. This will to require you to remove the parking-brake pedal (gravity is your parking brake now, and frankly, it'll work pretty well) and maybe more.

Then, there's the depth. Bigger wheels are usually wider as well. Wider tires run into interference issues either with the outside fender lip or the inside. The brake booster isn't usually an issue on these trucks, but with a wide wheel and tire up front with a body drop, adjustments may need to be made.

The part that not many people talk about is building the wheel tubs to accommodate turning. There's a reason for that. The natural assumption is that an adjustable suspension can just lift the front of the truck up to turn. Yes, that is a perfectly reasonable theory. However, in practice, no one wants to do that on every turn. On top of that, what about slow turns? Are you constantly raising and lowering the truck? Of course not. You didn't build the thing to look like it was lifted.

In addition, if it's body dropped, it's going to be tucking a lot of rim. That means the truck has to be lifted super high to clear them, and even then it's not convenient. Instead, just build the wheel tubs to accommodate lower ride heights. Plan ahead so that if you're going to put your truck into hovercraft mode, you'll still be able to swerve to avoid something in the road. It seems obvious, but it's not something that many people think about during their builds.

This four-door Tahoe required a lot of work to lay down on top of those big billet wheels. (Photo Courtesy Switch Suspension)

CHAPTER 11

Body Drops

There are trucks that are low, and then there are trucks that are *really* low. The difference is often in the body. There's only so far you can go when lowering or bagging a truck. Once the frame hits the ground, that's it.

What if there was a way to get even lower? That's what a body drop is all about, and there are primarily three different ways to get there.

What Is a Body Drop?

First, let's define the term. A body drop is what it sounds like: the body of the vehicle is dropped down over the frame. The goal is to place the body of the ride closer to the ground than the frame.

Let's put it another way. Get on your hands and knees by the door of the truck and then look at it from the side. See how the frame is lower than the cab? That gap (the few inches that make up where the bottom of the cab starts and the bottom of the frame starts) is what makes up a body drop. Ideally, the rocker panel (or even farther if you're willing to cut into the body) will lay on the ground (or really close to it) as a result.

Why would anyone want to do this kind of thing? Trucks sitting on the frame look pretty good. It's been standard for a long time now, and it's relatively easy to accomplish. Truck builders in the 1990s wanted to do something different. They knew about the hot rodders of days past who "channeled" their cars to cover up the frame. Why couldn't they do the same thing to their trucks? Then, instead of a boring frame on the ground, they'd have a painted surface. How cool would that be?

The answer was "very cool, thank you." Soon, a body drop became the next step for anyone laying frame. In addition, the wheel is tucked more that way. It's a very good look overall. Oh, and it's a lot easier to do with a truck than it is with a car because the cab and bed are separate. Lucky you.

So, how is a body drop accomplished? There are three main methods. No matter which one is chosen (or what combination of the three), two things remain constant: the front frame horns must also be modified to accommodate the body drop, and the bed must be dropped as well. Otherwise, it's up to you how you do the cab.

This particular truck, a 1995 Silverado, was set up so that the body sat about 1/4 inch off the ground, while the frame laid hard. This way, the frame (the stronger part) could take more abuse than the sheet metal.

Z-ing the Frame

If you were building a 1960–1987 Chevy truck and doing a body drop, things would look a lot different. For those trucks, the front crossmember is mammoth and is the primary thing that gets in the way. The frame itself, comparatively, isn't that big of a deal. Just find a way to pull the crossmember up 1-1/2 to 2 inches, and you might not even need to body drop the truck. The body is only an inch or so off the ground anyway.

In those trucks, there's a fix: get a new crossmember. They unbolt and bolt back in, making it a job that can be done with a cherry picker and an afternoon. It's easy(ish). However, you're not building one of those trucks.

The 1988–1998 Chevy and GMCs also have a problem with the front crossmember hanging lower than the body, but it's not as large of a variance (3/4 inch or so). Unfortunately, a smaller crossmember can't be installed because it's part of the frame. That means you have to accommodate for that crossmember to body drop the truck enough to actually lay body.

There are two ways to do this. The first way is to body drop the entire truck the amount that it would take to compensate for the front crossmember. The second way is to "Z" the frame.

The basic idea is pretty simple. Cut out the section of the frame behind the front crossmember but before the cab and do the same at the radiator supports. Then, lift the front crossmember the required amount and weld it all back in place. Step-by-step sequences under the heading "Performing a Stock-Floor Body Drop" show this later in this chapter. It is accomplished by first placing a 3/4-inch piece of square tubing between the frame and the jig before welding everything in place. However, if you're going another route, consider Z-ing the frame. It puts everything on more stable ground and looks a lot better too. ■

Traditional Body Drops

Traditional body drops were how builders began experimenting with the idea. Some hot rodders referred to it as "channeling" a truck. However, channeling is a very different thing in the world of body drops.

A traditional body drop is accomplished by cutting out the perimeter of the interior floor of the truck, lowering the cab down until it reaches the desired finish point, and then welding filler panels in place to clean up the gap that is left behind. It's pretty straightforward but has a few pros and cons.

On the positive side, it's relatively easy. The frame doesn't need to be messed with at all, which means that clearance issues with the transmission, engine, exhaust, etc. aren't as much of a problem. If they're ambitious, some builders can pull this off in a weekend.

Many people who perform a traditional body drop do so because they

This crew-cab dually has a traditional body drop. It tucked 19-inch wheels just fine and looked great on the ground.

On the interior of this truck, the seat mounts have been cut down substantially to increase headroom. The floor is much higher too.

want to go to the point where the cab meets the frame and beyond.

Some trucks have a pinch molding on the bottom of the cab that joins two panels. If a truck is body dropped so that the pinch molding is on the ground, it's "laying pinch." If the truck doesn't have pinch molding or you go past it to the rocker panels, then it's "laying rocker." If you go even further, to where the rocker is cut off entirely so that the bottom of the door is on the ground, you're "laying door."

It's often easier to get a truck to lay door or beyond with a traditional body drop than channeling or with a stock floor, which is one reason why people do it. Alternatively, some people use a combination of the different methods when they're cutting into the body.

For the record, not many people do body drops beyond the rocker anymore, but it's still out there.

On the downside, a traditional body drop robs the driver of two things: legroom and headroom.

Since the floor is being raised, it makes sense that you'd lose some headroom up top. With a full-size truck, that's not a very big deal unless you're either a) tall or b) taking the body drop to the door. You probably already have a few inches to spare anyway. However, if you're going bigger, more will be lost, and it could become pretty cramped inside. The solution is to cut down the seat mounts. This returns some (or most) of the headroom, but it'll feel like you're sitting on the floor. That's because you are.

That brings us back to the legroom issue. When sitting in a stock truck, your knees are bent at least slightly. By lowering the seats, your legs will no longer be bent, making them take up more space on the floor. The cab is also closer to the bottom of the pedals now, so you'll need to modify them to raise them. Even then, it might take some creative magic to fit in there correctly.

There are other issues, albeit minor ones. With a 5-speed transmission, the shifter can run into the dash because the distance between the floor and the dash is shorter. With a center console that goes under the dash (like is found in an Escalade or a Denali), that might have interference issues. In addition, you might find that your shins hit the dash, making it uncomfortable to drive.

Because of these issues, and further advancements in the world of body drops, not many folks are doing a traditional body drop anymore. Today's preference heavily leans toward a stock-floor body drop. That's not to say that you shouldn't do a traditional body drop—just be aware of the pros and cons.

Channeling

Channeling a truck takes the old hot rod concept to a different level. If the goal is to lower the cab down over the frame but not cut out the entire floor, why not cut out sections over the frame? You're not cutting out everything—just channels (hence the name).

So how does one get the drop? Cut the cab mounts off the frame, lower them the appropriate amount, and then weld them back in place. If they don't go down far enough, cut the mounts on the cab, remove a section of sheet metal, and weld them back into place. This can get the 2.75 inches or so that is needed to lay rocker pretty easily.

Now pre-bend the channels and cut them to size on the truck. This will have a nice, clean look instead of something that appears homemade. One thing to do to make it appear as if there isn't a channel in the carpet is to use sound-deadening material around the channel to build up the sides. It not only helps remove the extra heat from the exhaust being so close to the cab but also cuts down on noise.

Again, there are pros and cons.

On the positive side, it's better looking than a traditional body drop. It will still have most of the legroom, the headroom stays intact, and, with some careful application of sound-deadening material, it looks like it still has a stock floor.

The downsides depend on your height. A taller person may feel slighted at how much room is lost between their knees and the dash. There's a lot of cutting around the floor on the passenger's side to cover the catalytic converters (assuming that they aren't relocated entirely), and that can make it feel like the whole floor might as well just be cut out. It's a pretty tall channel too.

Admittedly, channeling is not ideal for every truck. The 1988–1998 trucks fall into this category. However, it's awesome on the 1999–2007 NBS trucks. The channels tend to get pretty high on OBS trucks, and although it's still better than a traditional body drop, it's not as nice as a stock floor. The catalytic converters need space, and the floor might have to be cut to fit them. With an extra-cab, it gets a bit tricky in the rear.

If you decide to go this route, there's some basic math to do to determine how tall the channels will be. Begin by taking a piece of square tubing and clamping it down to the bottom of the frame. It should be long enough that it extends past the rockers, and it will represent the ground when the frame sits down on it. Measure the distance between the bottom of the square tubing and the rocker. Let's call that A.

Next, measure from the top of the frame to the bottom of the floor. Remember to look for the actual floor, not a crossmember that hangs down lower. Call that B. What is left is the height of the channel (C).

Now, plug that into this equation:

$$A - B + 0.25 = C$$

Channeling a 1997 Chevrolet Silverado

The owner of this truck wanted a body drop, but was also 6 feet, 5 inches tall, so a traditional drop was out of the question. He decided to go with channeling because he could do it himself, and he didn't want to take the truck apart as far as would be required with a stock-floor body drop.

The truck is a 1997 Chevrolet Silverado with a Cadillac Escalade front clip and 22-inch Bonspeed wheels.

Teardown

1 *Remove anything that is not directly connected to the cab, including the bed (for accessibility), as well as the front clip (minus the core support).*

2 *Strip the interior of the truck, including the dashboard, carpet, seats, trim, etc. Basically, remove anything that could catch fire or is in the way.*

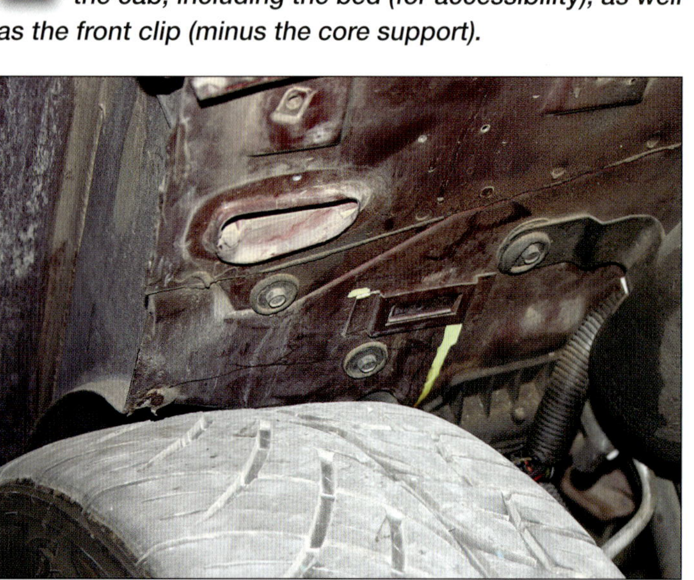

3 *This truck has been laid out so that the frame is on the ground. In this case, the tires touched the firewall, so it needs to be notched out. Using a yellow paint marker, mark the firewall. The idea is to add the amount of body drop being done to where it sits currently (assuming that it's on frame). In this case, that was 2¾ inches.*

Cutting the Firewall for Clearance

1 After an initial cut on the passenger's side, you can see from the inside where things need to be cut. There's a harness over there (the square box to the left) that will be rotated out of the way.

2 The passenger's side of the truck holds the air-conditioning system, and in this case, the fresh-air intake is in the way. Fortunately, it can be fixed by notching the box and sealing it with a plastic panel and some epoxy.

3 The firewall tubs are made from trailer fenders that can be picked up from any trailer-supply store. Using them as a template, trace the arc on the firewall for cutting.

Cutting the Firewall for Clearance *continued*

4 *Now, it has been welded into place with the new harness mount flipped 90-degrees. The owner had plans to smooth out the firewall later, so for the moment, brush-on seam sealer was placed over the seams to ensure that there wouldn't be leaks.*

5 *On the driver's side it's pretty much the same situation. However, this time, the body harness has to be taken into account, so it's rotated and moved slightly under the brake booster.*

Cutting the Core Support Mounts

1 *Looking at the passenger's side of the core support, the lower radiator hose is clearly in the way. Mark the frame for this so that it can be notched appropriately later.*

2 *Doing the core support mounts is straightforward. Mark the cut line, cut the frame with a Sawzall, and tack weld it into place. Cut a notch for the radiator hose as well. Then, gusset and weld everything up.*

Marking and Cutting the Channels

One way to know where the body is going to interfere with something (exhaust, frame, wiring, etc.) is to cut off a piece of 1-inch steel that is roughly 1/4 inch taller than the proposed body drop. This helps to compensate for the tighter clearances so that you will know where things will hit beforehand.

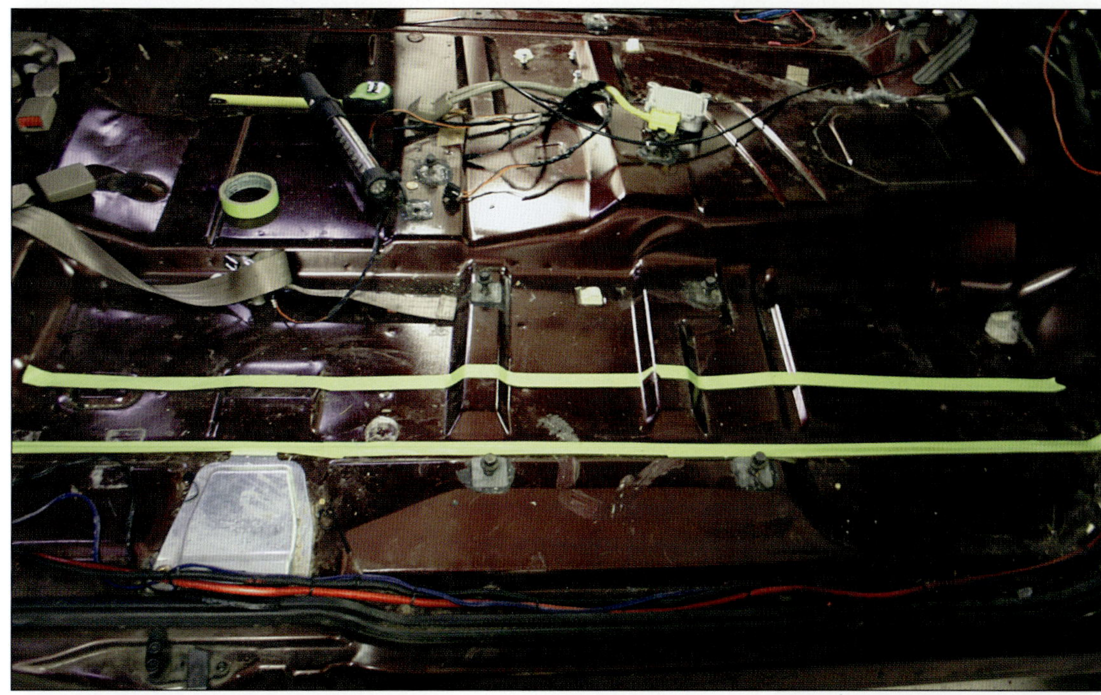

1 *Prior to cutting, mark the floor with masking tape so that it is clear where the channels will sit.*

2 *Once the truck is on jack stands with a spotter underneath, cut the channels. The spotter can make sure that the blade doesn't accidentally nick a brake line or anything else.*

Marking and Cutting the Channels *continued*

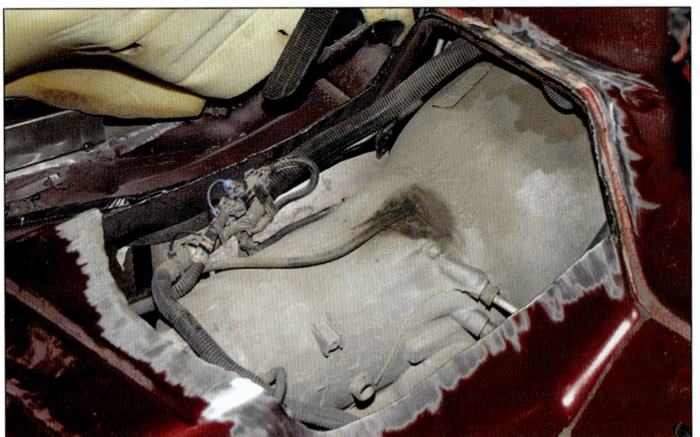

3 *Do the same around the transmission tunnel. Remove the hump and set it aside.*

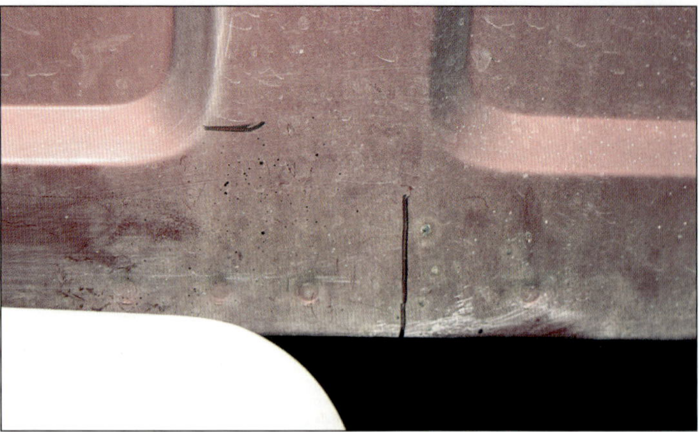

4 *The gas tank sits underneath the cab, so it has to be accommodated for as well. Mark the cab with a Sharpie and cut it out.*

Cutting the Cab Mounts

1 *If you look at the frame and the mount, there are two marks. These represent the amount of body drop that the truck will have. The idea is to cut off the mount, lower it so that what was the top line on the mount aligns with the lower mount on the frame, and then weld it in place.*

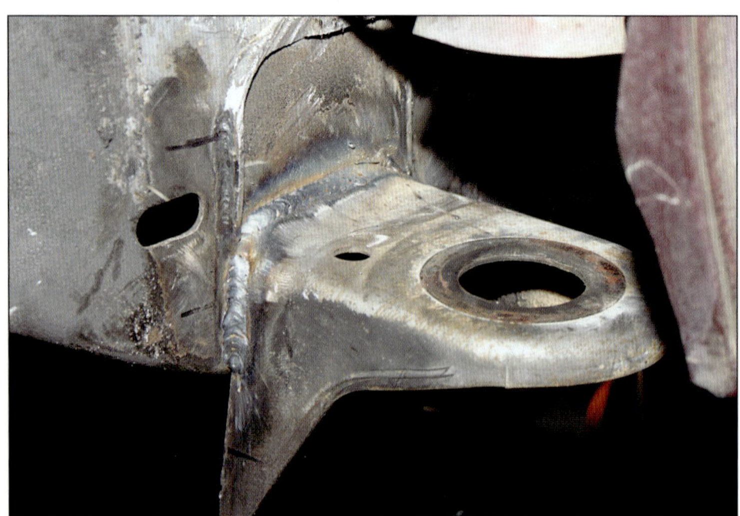

2 *Line up the mount and weld it in place. The old gussets need to be cut off the frame, and new ones need to be made that angle up instead.*

Installing the Channels

1 These channels were pre-bent by a local sheet-metal shop, which made life easier. Tack weld them into place, using a 1/2-inch spacer on top of the frame for added clearance.

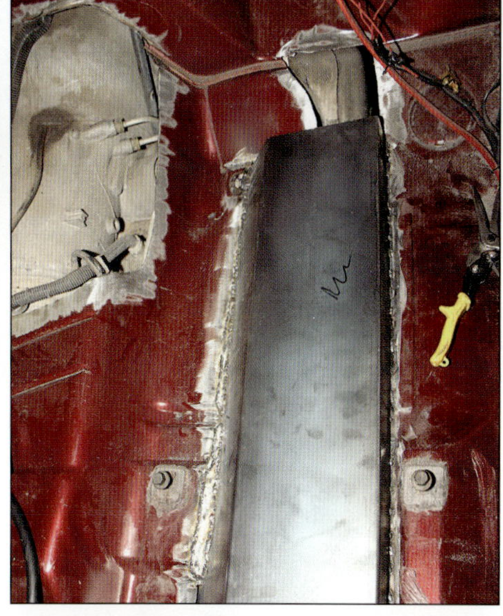

2 On the passenger's side, widen the channel to accommodate for the exhaust.

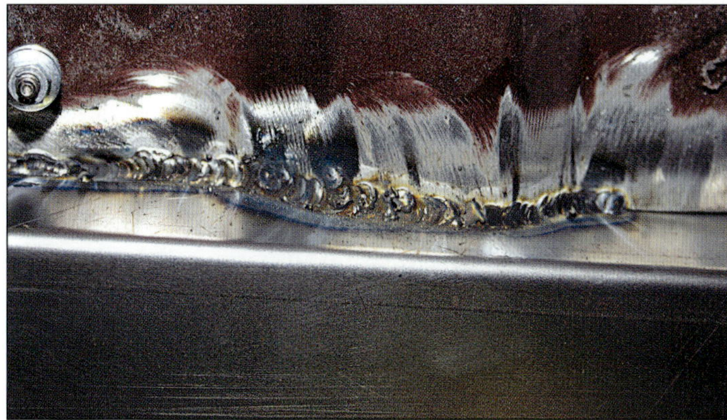

3 Once everything has been tacked in place, fully weld the panels in, ensuring that everything is nice and solid. Remove any excess steel on the underside of the truck.

4 Fabricate a new piece of sheet metal for the transmission hump and weld it into place. Apply seam sealer along all panel transitions between new and old sheet metal.

Installing Sound Deadener

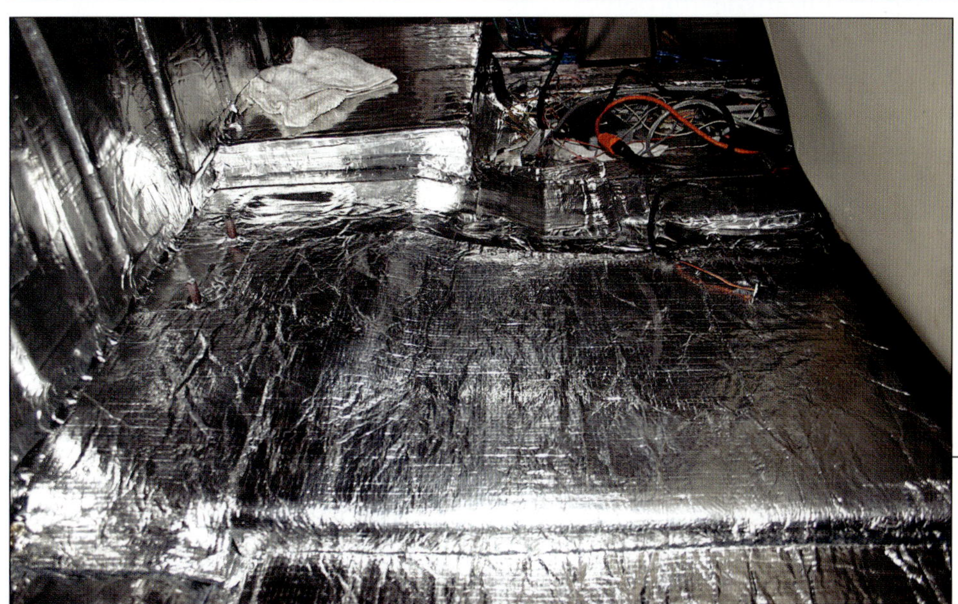

1 The finishing touch was applying sound deadener to the entire cab. Not only does this cut down on sound but it also helps to insulate from heat, which is a big deal when the cab is so much closer to the ground and the exhaust is closer to the floor.

Installing Sound Deadener *continued*

2 *Run any wiring (for the stereo and the like) alongside the channels and hold it down using strips of sound deadener. This also helped later with the installation of carpet and made the transitions look smoother.*

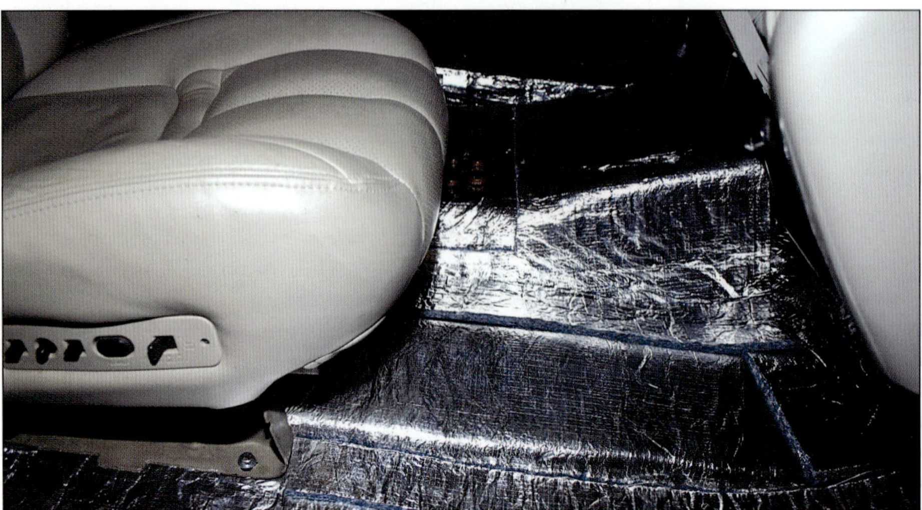

3 *The seat fits well and has no issues moving back and forth. There's plenty of room for carpet too.*

Stock-Floor Body Drops

A stock-floor body drop has a bit of a misleading name. For the most part, the idea is to keep the floor of the truck as factory as possible. However, the floor will definitely not be stock. From the transmission tunnel to the gas tank (and maybe even the driveshaft), modifications will be involved. However, it will look mostly stock overall.

This type of body drop involves completely disassembling the truck so that all that is left is a chassis. Then, after putting it on a jig, cut out the middle sections of the frame underneath the cab. New, shorter frame rails are stitched into the existing chassis, and the cab mounts are lowered the desired amount of the body drop. This creates a floor that's mostly stock, one that the stock carpet should be able to be reinstalled onto.

There are a few things to think about with a stock floor (or any body drop) on one of these trucks. If a motor swap is happening, do that before laying the truck on the ground. The clearance around the transmission may change, and it would be inefficient to do that work twice. The same goes for adjusting anything on the firewall, or if wiring needs to move. The other hitch is a bit more important.

Technically, laying frame on these trucks usually means that the front crossmember sits on the ground, as does the rear half of the frame under the cab. However, it's not actually level. That's because the front crossmember hangs about 3/4 inch lower than the rest of the frame. So, if you're doing a body drop, factor that in as well.

It's easiest to manage this with a stock-floor body drop, since everything already has been set up on a jig anyway. Otherwise, some different math will have to be done.

Regardless, this method of body drop is the most popular to do on these trucks. It's not easy, and it does require a lot of teardown, but the results are worth it.

Performing a Stock-Floor Body Drop

Before diving in, remember that there's a lot involved with this job. It requires at least twice the space that it takes to store the truck, as it will be in three parts (chassis, bed, and cab), and all of those components have to go somewhere. It is also important to be confident in your welding abilities. This is your frame, after all, and screwing that up is an expensive proposition. However, with careful planning, things will go just fine.

Initial Teardown

1 *Just a few weeks after the truck had airbags installed, it was torn down all over again for the body drop at Lowboy Motorsports.*

2 *Removing the cab from the frame is much easier with a lift. Without one, you need to get creative.*

3 *Using a wood block, a jack, four jack stands, and some steel tubing, the cab of this truck was lifted off the frame*

4 *After the rear wheels were removed, the chassis was slid forward using a pair of jacks on the rear end.*

Setting the Chassis on the Jig

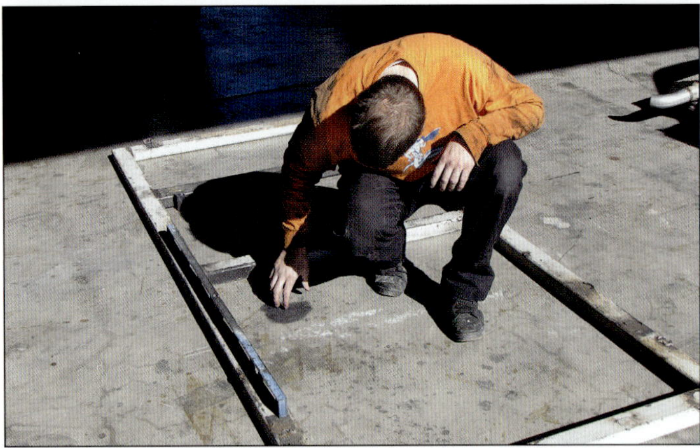

1 The jig itself is a simple structure of rectangular tubing that is welded to various specifications. After it has been leveled, the frame can be set on top of it.

2 A 3/4-inch spacer is placed beneath the portion of the frame under the cab to accommodate for the front crossmember.

3 The chassis has been welded in place across the jig so that nothing shifts during the build process. This is critical. Without it, the frame will be out of square.

4 Some round tubing that's the same size as the hole in the cab mounts is welded into place.

Cutting the Stock Frame

1 The idea with the tubing is that the cab mounts are being lowered, and there needs to be a reference point for future measurements. The tubing serves as that reference point.

Cutting the Stock Frame *continued*

2 *With everything secured, remove the stock frame just forward of the front cab mounts and just behind the rears.*

3 *The resulting chassis is now in two pieces and ready for the new frame to be built.*

Installing the New Frame

1 *Cut each piece of the new 2x4 3/16-inch tubing on a bandsaw for accuracy.*

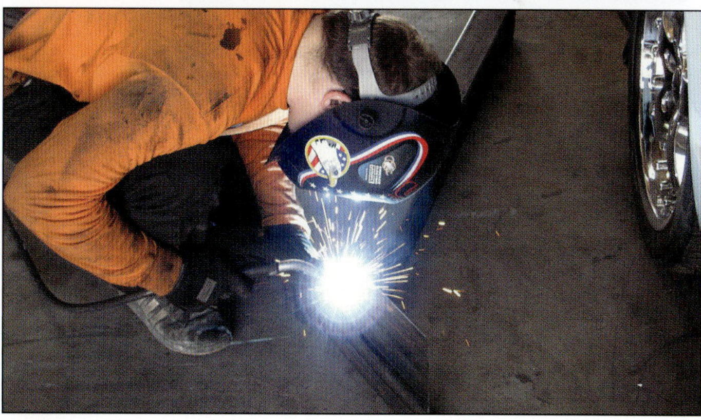

2 *There's a straight section and an angle up to meet the rear half. Weld these two pieces to match perfectly.*

3 *Weld these new frame sections into the chassis. This is the rear portion, and it's a fairly simple splice at this point.*

4 *In the front, it's more complicated. It'll take a compound-angle cut to line up everything. Perform measurements and do test fitting with some scrap steel. The gap on the left side of the photo will be addressed as well.*

Installing the New Frame

1 *Weld the first part of the frame into place. They're spliced, but it's still not a perfect connection yet.*

2 *Cut and weld an angled section of square tubing in place to fill in the transition between the new and old frame. Then, weld a fishplate across the entire section, tying it all together and making it extra strong.*

3 *Weld fishplates such as these at all of the connection points. They ensure that the joint is beefy and won't come apart.*

4 *The new cab mounts are straightforward. They're the same design as the originals, but some tweaks were made to the gussets to accommodate the new frame.*

5 *The new rear cab mounts are the same, and they tie into the forward bed mounts.*

Modifying the Cab Floor

1 After the cab has been test fitted onto the new frame, it's time to make some cuts. Notch the rear of the cab to clear the driveline. A plasma cutter makes quick work of the job.

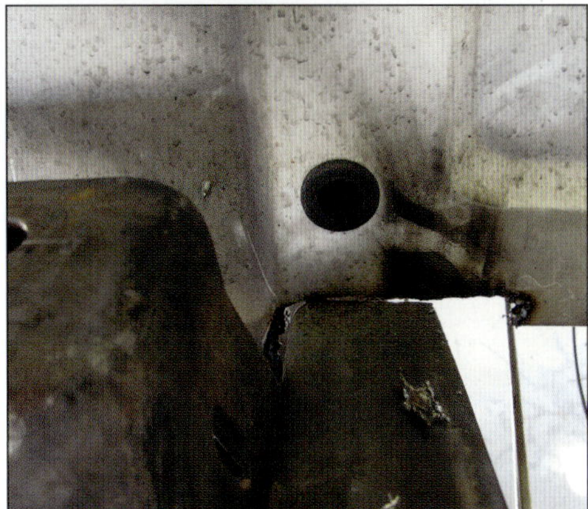

2 Make relief cuts for the new frame in the cab. They're tiny but necessary

3 The big spot to work on is the transmission tunnel. Keep the original sheet metal as a reference for everything new.

4 After doing some basic metalwork, test fit the panel in place. There will be gaps to fill, but so far, it's not much.

5 Tack weld the transmission cover into place for now. Soon, all of that sheet metal will be filled in with new stock.

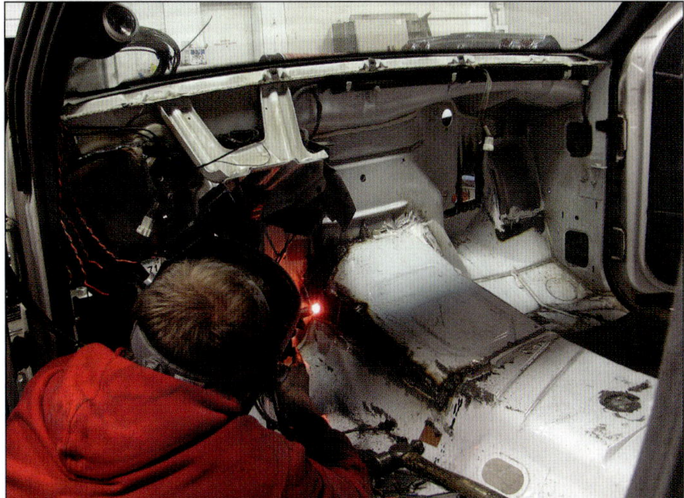

6 With the transmission properly clearanced, weld in the rest of the cover. Cut pieces of sheet metal and weld them into place.

Modifying the Cab Floor *continued*

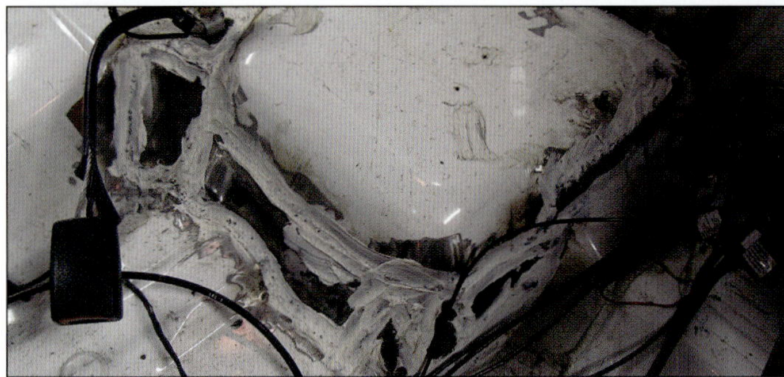

7 *Notch the cab for the gas tank as well. Once that's done, use seam sealer and prepare for the next part of the process.*

Tubbing the Firewall

1 *The truck now lays body on 20-inch wheels, but the tires hit the firewall. On top of that, the owner wants to run 22s in the future, so the firewall needs to be clearanced.*

2 *After taking measurements, use a piece of a sheet metal (a trailer fender in this case) to mark the cab for the new section.*

3 *After that's done, cut out the firewall using a cut-off wheel. Next, weld the trailer fenders into place, completing the task.*

4 *The team at Lowboy Motorsports fabricated this custom transmission crossmember with a clearance tube for the exhaust.*

Lowering the Core Support Mounts

1 *Before cutting the core support mounts, weld a piece of tubing between them. This ensures that the core supports are aligned when they're welded back in place.*

2 *Mark, cut, and tack weld the mounts into place. Note that the mounts were lowered an additional 3/4 inch to compensate for the front crossmember.*

3 *A radiator hose on the passenger's side needs extra space. To solve this problem, notch the frame. Weld a piece of plate into place.*

Finishing Touches

1 *Since this truck is keeping the rear bumper, the existing brackets needs to be modified to work. So, just like the core support, lower them the same amount and then weld them into place.*

Finishing Touches *continued*

2 *After the cab has been seam sealed, cover the entire thing with Dynamat Xtreme. It's a peel-and-stick process, and the result is reduced vibrations and less road noise.*

3 *Next, install Dynamat Xtremeliner (now Dynaliner) to add another sound-deadening layer and reduce heat in the cab. This is important because everything is so much closer to the floor.*

4 *Install the factory carpet back in. It's not a 100-percent perfect fit, but once the seats and trim are installed, you'd never know the difference.*

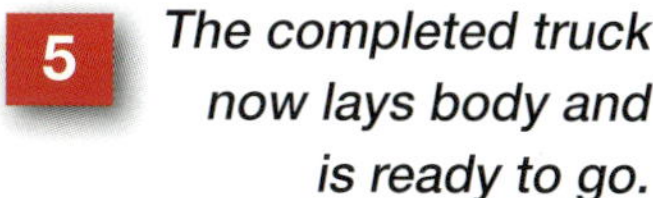

5 *The completed truck now lays body and is ready to go.*

It doesn't matter if you're doing a stock-floor body drop, traditional body drop, or channeling the truck, the bed needs a matching job. Essentially, this means cutting out the perimeter of the bed floor and raising it up the appropriate amount. If you're body dropping the truck 2¾ inches (which is fairly standard), raise the bed floor the same amount.

With that being said, there are other options. If a stock bed floor hasn't had anything cut out in the sheet metal for the bridge, consider body dropping the bed more to accommodate for that notch. That

When done, the bed can look just like this. Either cover everything with a bedliner or do the bodywork and paint it. It's your call.

may mean raising the floor 6 to 8 inches in total, which seems like a lot. However, spacers can then be added between the existing frame mounts and the bed floor to make up that difference.

Although raising the floor higher is a popular option, some people don't like it because it reduces useable hauling space. What's a truck bed for if it's not hauling large things, right?

To many, a stock bed floor (even if it's raised higher than stock) is a better look than a big hole in the bed, even if it's covered. Hey, the plan is to body drop the truck anyway. Will it really be hauling lumber?

There are multiple ways to do this job. Some builders prefer to drill out the welds on the bed sides, leaving just the box to work with. Others do their cuts in different ways to hide them. This is also a slightly different process on a stepside bed, as those bed sides are fiberglass, and there aren't any inner fenders to worry about. The way shown here is just one option, but it's good guidance for whichever way you choose.

Prepping the Bed

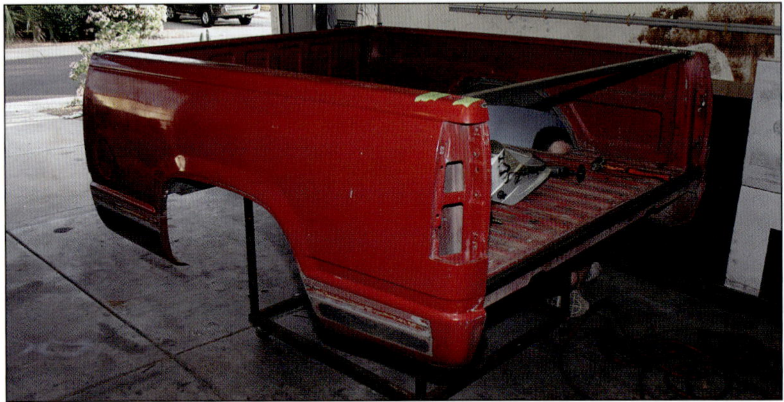

1 *Before starting, put the bed on a cart of some kind in case it needs to be moved. In addition, remove everything else, including taillights, tailgate, and a tonneau or shell (if the truck has one).*

2 *Weld some square tubing at the top of the bed by the tailgate and again toward the bottom. This ensures that the whole thing doesn't "parallelogram" on you when the structure of the bed is cut out.*

3 *Note the measurements between the bed rails. Use them for future reference when those bars are cut out. In addition, measure from the bottom of the floor to the top of the bed in multiple spots, so that you know when things are done properly.*

Taking Measurements and Marking Cuts

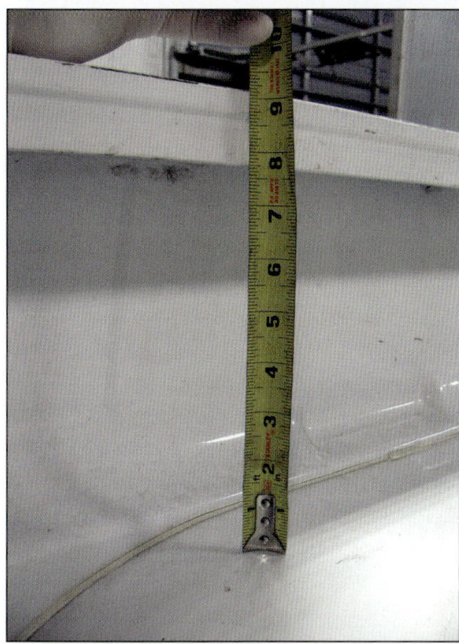

1 *Some people run wide wheels and have to cut out the stock rear fender wells. Others don't run wide wheels and leave the rear fender wells stock. If you want to go the original route, the maximum body drop possible on the bed without modifying the fenders is about 7.75 inches.*

2 *The bed side supports also have to be removed. They'll be lengthened to match the new depth of the bed. Keep them on the truck. Otherwise, the bed sides will flap when driving.*

3 *Any surface that's going to get welded needs to have the paint removed. It's simple enough to do with a die grinder and an 80-grit Roloc disc.*

4 *The same goes for where the bed is going to go. In this case, it will be re-welded at the stake pocket, so the paint is removed, and a mark is placed at 7.75 inches.*

5 *The same paint removal process happens at the back bed wall. Once the floor is dropped, everything will be welded in place there.*

Cutting and Welding the Bed

1 *You most likely want to hide the cuts wherever possible, and one easy way to do that is to hide them under the bed rail. Make the initial cut across the length of the bed with a cut-off wheel.*

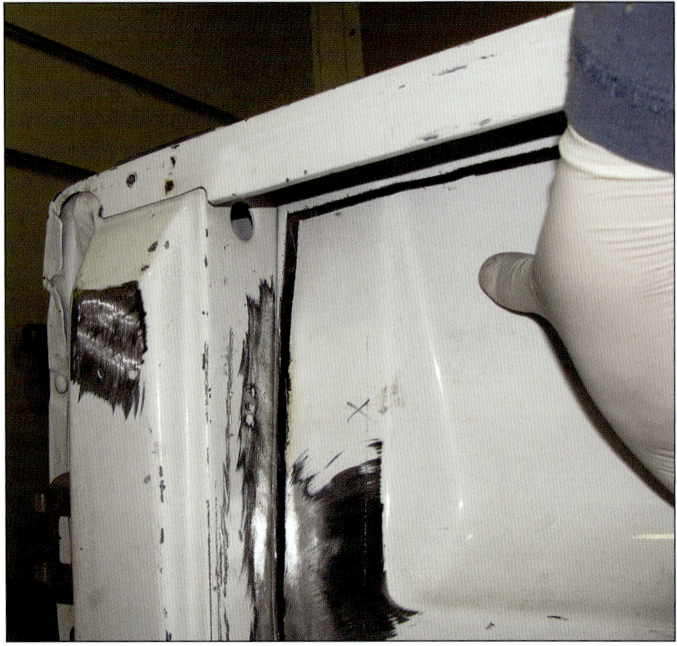

2 *Vertical cuts are made the same way. Again, they're hidden in the sides and by the stake pockets.*

3 *Then comes the second cut on the bed sides. This will remove 7.75 inches from the area so that the two halves can meet and be welded up.*

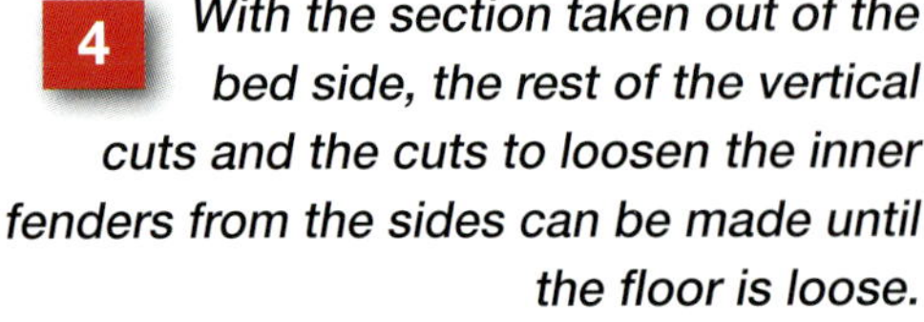

4 *With the section taken out of the bed side, the rest of the vertical cuts and the cuts to loosen the inner fenders from the sides can be made until the floor is loose.*

5 *Once the floor is raised up, the first thing to tack into place is the fender wells to the bed floor. This provides a good place to start solidifying the structure. Then, weld up everything else.*

Miscellaneous Modifications

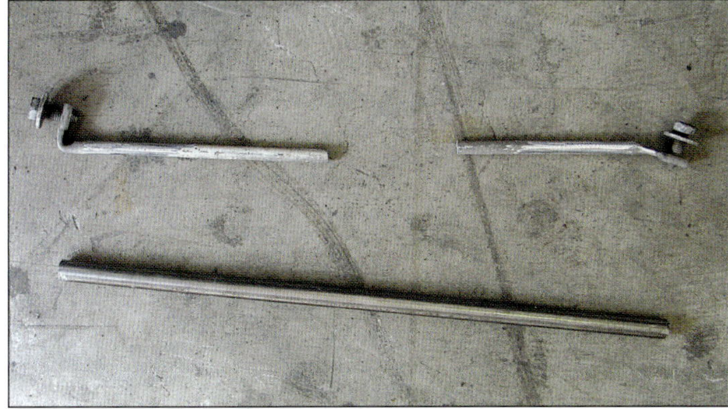

1 *The bed side supports need to be lengthened. The easiest way to do this is to cut the original in half. Then, slide some tubing over it that fits snugly.*

2 *Tack weld the tubing in place, remove it from the truck, finish weld it, and reinstall it.*

Miscellaneous Modifications *continued*

3 *The bed has been body dropped 7.75 inches, but the notch would still hit the bed floor unless this support was removed. After it was cut out, everything cleared.*

4 *To make up the 5-inch difference in the bed floor height, spacers and threaded rod were used to bolt the bed in place. Nicer models can also be built with a standard bolt and nut.*

5 *For now, the truck was done. It drives great and has an excellent new stance. It was painted shortly after this photo was taken.*

Source Guide

Air Lift Performance
800-248-0892
airliftperformance.com

Air Zenith
3651 W. Ali Baba Ln. Suite 107
Las Vegas, NV 89118
702-270-7988
air-zenith.com

Arizona High Test
4043 W. Kitty Hawk Way Suite 1
Chandler, AZ 85226
Instagram: @arizona_high_test

Ashcroft
250 E. Main St.
Stratford, CT 06614
203-378-8281
ashcroft.com

Autometer
413 W. Elm St.
Sycamore, IL 60178
866-248-6357
autometer.com

AVS
4555 N. Cedar Ave.
Fresno, CA 93726
559-486-5444
avsontheweb.com

Bag Riders
208 Flynn Ave. Suite 2C
Burlington, VT 05401
844-404-7344
bagriders.com

BellTech
300 W. Pontiac Way
Clovis, CA 93612
800-445-3767
belltech.com

Carolina Kustoms
6600 NE Columbia Blvd.
Portland, OR 97218
503-954-1369
carolinakustoms.com

Choppin' Block Chassis Products (CBC)
5553 W. Barstow Ave.
Fresno, CA 93722
559-275-2901
cbcpro.com

Chris Alson's Chassisworks
8661 Younger Creek Dr.
Sacramento, CA 95828
888-388-0297
cachassisworks.com

Continental
continental-industry.com

Cool Cars Engineering
7514 Preston Hwy.
Louisville, KY 40219
502-969-7600
coolcars.org

D2 Racing
2435 S. Alston Ave.
Durham, NC 27713
919-544-4171
d2racing.com

Dakota Digital
4510 W. 61st St. N.
Sioux Falls, SD 57107
605-332-6513
dakotadigital.com

Dino's Chevy Only
dinoschevyonly.com

Dynamat
513-860-5094
dynamat.com

EBC Brakes
6180 S. Pearl St.
Las Vegas, NV 89120
702-826-2400
ebcbrakes.com

Elevated Concepts Inc.
Hayden, ID
elevatedconceptsinc.com

Firestone
800-888-0650
firestoneip.com

Flo Airride Mfg
951-249-6478
floairride.com

Frontier Shop Supplies
4551 E. Ivy St.
Suite 101
Mesa, AZ 85205
480-981-1126
frontiershopsupplies.com

GlowShift Gauges
444 Commerce Ln. Suite A
West Berlin, NJ 08091
856-768-8300
glowshiftdirect.com

Grainger
800-472-4643
grainger.com

GrantFab
530-255-4712
grantfab.com

Grunion Customs
13011 N. Cave Creek Rd.
Phoenix, AZ 85022
602-258-0088
grunionfabrication.com

Heidts
800 Oakwood Rd.
Lake Zurich, IL 60047
800-841-8188
heidts.com

KP Components
8661 Younger Creek Dr.
Sacramento, CA 95828
888-388-0299
kpcomponents.com

Kwix UK
330 Four Oaks Rd.
Walton Summit,
Preston, PR5 8AP
United Kingdom
01772 695 697
kwixuk.com

Little Shop Mfg.
150 Mahr Ave.
Lawrenceburg, TN 38464
littleshopmfg.com

LG Billet USA
133 E. Comstock Dr. Suite 1
Chandler, AZ 85225
lgbilletusa.com

Lowboy Motorsports
1045 W. Broadway Rd. Suite 4
Mesa, AZ 85210
480-717-9256
lowboymotorsports.com

McGaughys
4603 E. Vine Ave.
Fresno, CA 93725
559-226-8196
mcgaughys.com

Metalox Fabrication
8615 W. Kelton Ln. Suite 305
Peoria, AZ 85382
623-308-1170
Instagram: @metaloxfab

Oasis Manufacturing
23011 Alcalde Dr. Suite P
Laguna Hills, CA 92653
888-966-2747
oasismfg.com

Parker
800-272-7537
parker.com

Pro Performance
7931 E. Pecos Rd. Suite 198
Mesa, AZ 85212
480-420-8175
azproperformance.com

QA1
9574 217th St. W.
Lakeville, MN 55044
952-985-5675
qa1.net

Roadster Shop
28775 N. Rte. 83
Mundelein, IL 60060
847-949-7637
roadstershop.com

RedHead Steering Gears
4302 B St. NW
Auburn, WA 98001
800-808-1148
redheadsteeringgears.com

RideTech
350 S. St. Charles Street
Jasper, IN 47546
812-481-4787
ridetech.com

Rigid Tools
400 Clark St.
Elyria, OH 44035
800-474-3443
ridgid.com

Slam Specialties
5845 E. Terrace Ave.
Fresno, CA 93727
888-352-5225
slamspecialties.com

SMC Pneumatics
3810 Prospect Ave. Unit A
Yorba Linda, CA 92886
714-312-5419
smcpneumatics.com

Street Scene
365 McCormick Ave.
Costa Mesa, CA 92626
888-477-0707
streetsceneeq.com

Swagelok
swagelok.com

Switch Suspension
2340 W. Broadway Rd. Suite 105
Mesa, AZ 85202
800-928-1984
switchsuspension.com

Texas Speed & Performance
101 Velocity Dr., Suite 100
Georgetown, TX 78628
512-863-0900
texas-speed.com

Toyo Tire & Rubber Company
toyotires.com

Tuckers Classic Auto Parts
800-544-1955
tuckersparts.com

Universal Air Suspension
463 W. Highland Ave.
San Bernardino, CA 92405
800-864-2470
universalair.com

Viair
15 Edelman
Irvine, CA 92618
949.585.0011
viaircorp.com